Transforming Leadership

TRANSFORMATIONS
THE EPISCOPAL CHURCH IN THE 21ST CENTURY

Transforming Leadership

KATHERINE TYLER SCOTT

Church Publishing
NEW YORK

Cover design by Stefan Killen Design
Study guide and interior design by Vicki K. Black

Library of Congress Cataloging-in-Publication Data
Tyler Scott, Katherine
Transforming leadership / Katherine Tyler Scott.
    p.   cm.
Includes bibliographical references.
ISBN 978-0-89869-599-1 (pbk.)
1. Christian leadership. 2. Christian leadership—Episcopal Church.
3. Change—Religious aspects—Christianity. 4. Church renewal.
5. Church renewal—Episcopal Church. I.Title.
BV652.1.T95 2010
254'.03—dc22
                    2009044092

Printed in the United States of America

Church Publishing, Incorporated
445 Fifth Avenue
New York, New York 10016

www.churchpublishing.org

5 4 3 2 1

Contents

a note from the publisher

This series emerged as a partnership between
the Office of Mission of the Episcopal
Church and Church Publishing, as a contribution to the mission of the church in a new
century. We would like to thank James
Lemler, series editor, for bringing the initial
idea to us and for facilitating the series. We
also want to express our gratitude to the
Office of Mission for two partnership
grants: the first brought all the series authors
together for two creative days of brain-
storming and fellowship; and the second is
helping to further publicize the books of the
series to the clergy and lay people of the
Episcopal Church.

Series Preface

"Be ye transformed" (KJV). "Be transformed by the renewing of your minds" (NRSV). "Fix your attention on God. You'll be changed from the inside out" (*The Message*). Thus St. Paul exhorted the earliest Christian community in his writing to the Romans two millennia ago. This exhortation was important for the early church and it is urgent for the Episcopal Church to heed as it enters the twenty-first century. Be transformed. Be changed from the inside out.

Perhaps no term fits the work and circumstances of the church in the twenty-first century better than "transformation." We are increasingly aware of the need for change as we become ever more mission-focused in the life of the church, both internationally and domestically. But society as a whole is rapidly moving in new directions, and mission cannot be embraced in an unexamined way, relying on old cultural and ecclesiastical stereotypes and assumptions.

This new series, *Transformations: The Episcopal Church in the 21st Century*, addresses these issues in realistic and hopeful ways. Each book focuses on one area within the Episcopal Church that is urgently in need of transformation in order for the church to be effective in the twenty-first century: vocation, evangelism, preaching, congregational

life, getting to know the Bible, leadership, Christian formation, worship, and stewardship. Each volume explains why
a changed vision is essential, gives robust theological and
biblical foundations, offers guidelines to best practices and
positive trends, describes the necessary tools for change, and
imagines how transformation will look.

In this volume Katherine Tyler Scott looks at leadership for the church in a new century, which looks different
even as it embodies traditions and practices from the past.
She notes that the recovery of a theology of baptism has
sent shock waves through the Episcopal Church, over-
turning settled views of ministry and precipitating new
models of leadership. Questioning and renegotiating the
authority, roles, responsibilities, and relationships between
lay and ordained leaders has become the order of the day.
As a result there is greater pressure on leaders and new
opportunities for service and transformation. The stakes
are high as mission and mission-focused congregations
require innovative and skilled leaders.

Like Christians in the early church, today we live in a
secular culture that can be apathetic and even hostile to
Christianity. Living in a setting where people are not
familiar with the message or narrative of Christian believing
requires new responses and new kinds of mission for the
Body of Christ. We believe this is a hopeful time for spiritual seekers and inquirers in the church. The gospel itself is
fresh for this century. God's love is vibrant and real; God's
mission can transform people's hopes and lives. Will we
participate in the transformation? Will we be bearers and
agents of transformation for others? Will we ourselves be
transformed? This is the call and these are the urgent questions for the Episcopal Church in the twenty-first century.

But first, seek to be transformed. Fix your attention on
God. You'll be changed from the inside out.

JAMES B. LEMLER, *series editor*

Preface

I began this longer-than-planned-for journey of writing and contributing to Church Publishing's Transformations series with a passion about leadership development and a strong belief that the times in which we live are calling forth the unique charism of the Episcopal Church. My belief and passion are stronger and my commitment even deeper now. In times of great complexity, confusion, and anxiety, we need knowledgeable, thoughtful, responsible action from leaders who are capable of responding responsibly to the adaptive challenges we face. We are in such a time, and the question is whether our historical lack of attention to the development of this kind of leadership has left us ill-prepared. The Protestant churches have many exemplary leaders—a few are cited in this book—but many more are needed. Leadership does not take place in a cultural vacuum, nor does preparation occur through osmosis. The times in which we live demand the moral responsibility of accurately reading reality and of being intentional in preparing leaders for a different and emerging context.

In heightening our awareness of the significant, seismic shifts taking place, we will be better equipped to analyze what they mean for our religious institutions that once were at the center of civic life but are now on the margin. This is one more contribution to a several decades-old conversation shaped by these shifts. Ministry and authority are no longer resident in just one individual. Clergy and laity share responsibility for leadership and ministry; all share responsibility for the wise and judicious use of their God-given authority. Power is not just perceived as the possession of a few; it is now the currency of many. It is this new view of leadership that will enable the church to grow in strength and in stature.

The new paradigm of leadership being shaped by laity and clergy, students and academics, educators and practitioners is the subject of this book. The first chapter introduces the context in which the conversation on leadership is continuing and provides a reason for the sense of urgency to develop a different kind of leadership able to engage with the deeper strata of change called transformation. Chapter 2 describes the predominant and emerging paradigms of leadership and the dramatic shift away from the toxic features of the traditional structure of church life and the leadership cultivated by it. A brief look at the challenges and potential of the Episcopal Church "on the margin" follows in chapter 3. Chapter 4 introduces several levels of parish culture and the leadership each requires for transformation. The last chapter addresses the vocational elements of leadership, and the vital practices that prepare leaders for a new reality.

It is my hope that this offering and the Transformations series will invite even more voices into this conversation and strengthen the commitment of the church to passionately invest in transforming the views and practices of leadership. May the Episcopal Church recognize its gift and unique call in bringing about this transformation.

Acknowledgments

Writing is both a solitary and communal enterprise. It is the writer who singularly puts pen to paper or finger to key, but there are a host of others who help to move the process from idea to reality. In so many ways the writing of a book takes a village.

For their passion about mission and foresight to offer this series, I thank Jim Lemler and Cynthia Shattuck; for Cynthia's guidance and ability to evoke contributions from such a diverse group, and for Vicki Black's editorial expertise, I give thanks.

I am indebted to the many lay and clergy leaders who shared their stories, and to Matthew Price and Kirk Hadaway for sharing their research data.

I am grateful to my colleagues at Ki ThoughtBridge, who help to create an environment in which my experience and knowledge of leadership development continues to evolve and contributes to worthy work. And I give thanks for the Episcopal Church, in which I have had so many opportunities to serve with great leaders.

Most of all I thank all of my family, especially Fred, for his unwavering love and encouragement; Frederick and Ava, for their support; and Isabella, whose joy of discovery reminds us all of the true Source of our gifts.

chapter one

A Time of No Longer and Not Yet

Well-defined self in a leader—what I call self-differentiation—is not only critical to effective leadership, it is precisely the leadership characteristic that is most likely to promote the kind of community that preserves the self of its members. —Edwin H. Friedman

"Can you help us?"

The question was plaintively expressed by the voice on the line after revealing an all-too-familiar situation. A midsized Episcopal parish in the northeast, nestled in a suburban area described as having the greatest population growth in decades, was experiencing a dramatic loss of members. The once slow decline in membership had become more noticeable in the previous year, when fifty congregants, many of whom were considered pillars within the congregation and in the larger community, left. The initial explanation for this mass exodus was unresolved conflict over the direction of the parish's programs, a decline in pledges, and shifting demographics. In the course of asking more probing questions, serious concerns surfaced about the perceived autocratic and imperious leadership style of the rector.

The rector's ultimate response to any congregational conflict was to state in various ways his positional power. "I am the rector" was a refrain used to trump any dissent or discord. His leadership style created divisions between the newer and the longer-term members. Those with little or no history of the parish seemed content and were impervious to the dissension; those with a lengthy history and more involvement were notably discontent and more expressive of their unhappiness. The fault lines within the congregation had begun to affect relationships between congregants, and rumors about the parish's problems seeped out into community, tarnishing its once stellar reputation.

Disagreement or criticism was deemed to be a personal attack; the rector was portrayed as a victim by those who supported him and a manipulator by those who disagreed with his actions. The consequence was an even deeper division within the congregation, with members taking sides and evolving into opposing camps of "us" and "them." The departure of a number of parish leaders in a short time created more fear and anxiety and a bunker mentality in the vestry, the one group that could be expected to exert leadership in this crisis. Their behavior served to escalate the hostile, defensive communication already tearing the congregation apart.

Answering their initial question—*"Can you help us?"*— meant asking more probing questions of clergy and lay leadership. For example:

* What is the current parish culture?
* How would you describe the relationships between lay and clergy leaders?
* How are authority and dependency handled?

* Are there "responsible critics"? How are they perceived and treated?
* How has the congregation confronted similar problems in the past?
* What is the congregation's mission and vision? How are they expressed?

An articulation of questions such as these could have led this congregation to a constructive discussion and problem-solving process. It might have helped those remaining congregants with unquestioned loyalty to the parish and its rector realize that a different kind of support, other than taking sides and demonizing the dissidents, was needed. The ability to identify, listen to, and address the concerns of those who expressed their displeasure could have helped the vestry and other congregational leaders obtain more timely professional help for both their priest and their community of faith. In this case the vestry leaders contributed to the polarization by encircling the priest and erecting a "no criticism" zone around themselves. Anyone who differed with their opinions or who were critical of the rector's behavior was not taken seriously, and marginalized.

> An unsafe place is any place in which our first-order experience is considered to be invalid, irrelevant, or untrue. It is disturbing to be in a situation in which we do not feel heard. Usually, in such a case, we do not trust what we are experiencing as real. This can be any place in which we feel our experience needs to be explained and defended rather than accepted and actively inquired into. —*Michael Jones*

So the answer to this parish's initial question was not simple. The congregation had become locked into a cycle of insularity that did not permit much self-examination, new learning, or corrective intervention. By the time the vestry and rector did seek outside assistance the request for help came more from a need to prove the rightness and wrongness of aggrieved parties than from a desire to change the pernicious behaviors that were damaging to the remaining community.

According to the Faith Communities Today (FACT) studies conducted by the Hartford Institute for Religious Research in 2001 and 2005, a large percentage of conflict occurring in Episcopal churches stems from the leadership style of the priest. The leadership style of the priest determines a congregation's perception of the roles and responsibilities of clergy, church staff, and laity. It is clergy leadership that enables a congregation to form and strengthen itself as a community and to understand the larger context in which parish life exists. Perceiving the larger context leads to a clearer understanding of the forces that affect congregational life and leadership. It also gives wiser guidance about how a parish can respond to a larger truth.

----

the larger context

Like so many other institutions, the church is not immune from the current seismic shifts taking place nationally and globally. Experts in every field recognize that we are in a period of such rapid and complex change that it is comparable to historical periods in which new epochs of human understanding emerged. This is a time that can be compared to the fourth century, when human beings witnessed the triumph of Christianity, and to the seventeenth century, which introduced the Modern Age.

During the fourth century human understanding of the Divine, and the relationship between the Divine and human beings, profoundly changed. For God so loved the world that he sent his only Son to redeem it?! What wondrous Love was this? The birth and ministry of Jesus transformed reality, a reality many found hard to accept. To believe that salvation came from being the recipient of a Love so sacrificial and powerful that it transformed everyone and everything was liberating to some and threatening to others. The disciples and early converts to Christianity ushered in this new reality through the spiritual disciplines of storytelling, preaching, prayer, evangelism, and worship, practices that enabled them to embrace a new way of seeing and being that was so paradoxical and radical that to this day it continues to raise doubts and engender disbelief. The Good News is disturbing; it changes everything—it is transforming!

A similar sense of dissonance and disruption occurred during the seventeenth century, as the value of reason and rational thinking increased and the concepts of democracy and national sovereignty emerged. Diogenes Allen, Professor at Princeton Theological Seminary, described this period as a time when "all that had been thought to be true and valuable was set aside. However hallowed, respected, loved, intellectual integrity required it to be verified by the sovereign court of reason."[1] It was a revolutionary time in which different understandings and perceptions of what is true and real emerged. It was the beginning of the Scientific Age, the origins of a painful parting between theology and psychology, and the triumph of facts over faith. Like the present time, these two periods in history were times when fundamental assumptions and views about reality were questioned and changed.

Once again we are in another period of dramatic change and shift. Facts are still highly valued, but what has changed dramatically is our access to a vast quantity of information. We can instantly communicate with almost anyone, anywhere, through devices smaller than a postcard. Schedules and address books are stored in palm-sized instruments that organize and manage our time in every setting in which we operate. We can meet electronically, as we see and talk with colleagues, family, and friends via computers and phones. Every individual is a potential source, disseminator, and recipient of data. The leadership challenge today is not obtaining or receiving facts and information, it is discerning the veracity and meaning of them.

Churches are normally thought to be contemplative places of spiritual respite and havens of stability, but the rapidity and complexity of change is contributing to a different internal and external reality. The current context in which the church exists demands responses that seem antithetical to traditional practices of worship. If the younger generation finds its connections to one other and forms community through Facebook and YouTube, how does this affect the ways in which the church preaches, worships, evangelizes, and teaches? If people are twittering and tweeting with each other, how can this form of relationship and communication help them form a strong faith relationship to God and to a church? If individuals can go online and find information that helps them interpret the Bible, what does this mean for the preaching and teaching role of clergy? If congregants can retrieve information electronically in seconds, how might this affect what, how, and when clergy convey what they deem as most precious and essential in the Good News? If phenomena such as iChat and Skype continue to be significant modes for connection, relationship, and community, how does this affect the ways people create meaning within a parish culture?

When the first indicators of these huge changes began to surface, the Episcopal Church responded by clarifying its mission and reorganizing its ministries. The mantra of

Service, Worship, Evangelism, Education, and Prayer (SWEEP) swept through pews and sacristies in the 1970s and 1980s. Christian education was given greater importance and expanded beyond children's Sunday school to include more substantial adult education.

Perhaps the most notable catalyst and reaction to these changes and the subsequent breakdown of the old order is the theological and liturgical recovery of baptism. It has prompted a serious reexamination of Christian identity, mission, and practice, challenged conventional views of ordained and lay ministry, and changed traditional forms of worship. The idea of the ministry of all the baptized has significantly affected roles and responsibilities of clergy and laity, and transformed their relationships to one another.

At a Consortium of Endowed Episcopal Parishes preconference for clergy several years ago, the tensions and opportunities of implementing this new vision revealed some of the unresolved concerns that frequently arise in congregations, and can either lead to more creative forms of ministry or increased conflict and power struggles, including the meaning of vocation, the identity of the priesthood, the redistribution of power, the definition of community, and the meaning of "the ministry of all the baptized." These areas of concern within congregations are still in various states of discussion, redefinition, and renegotiation. Parish leaders and congregants are in varying degrees of being caught between verbal professions of shared leadership and the longstanding cultural norms and structures of a church that still often operates as if its ministers are only those wearing clerical collars. We live in a time of no longer and not yet.

Shared ministry between clergy and laity can be an enlivening force in church culture and structures when the right kind of leadership is practiced. When clergy and lay leadership have a clear, shared vision, can listen respectfully to one another, can invite participation from everyone, and exhibit congruence between word and deed, followers will develop the trust and loyalty, and engagement necessary for sustainable church growth and vitality.[2]

The ultimate sustainability of the church and the effectiveness of its mission and ministry in the world will depend on factors such as these. The key then is the capacity of clergy to establish healthy relationships of vocational interdependence rather than a vocational caste system that promotes elitism. Many parishes are still trying to figure out what this interdependence should look like and, more importantly, *how* to live it. This task will become more challenging as the church encounters even more shifts in the near future and experiences the resulting disequilibrium that always attends such changes. We will find that in this time and place of no longer and not yet are opportunities for transformation. In such times we must acknowledge change and prepare to respond responsibly. There are three changes that demand the immediate attention of the church.

A SHIFT IN DIVERSITY

A future wave of change that can either lift the church to new heights or leave it dashed on the shores of denial is the increased ethnic diversification in the general population. By 2050, Caucasians will no longer be the numerical majority in the United States. While the Episcopal Church is still struggling with what it means to fully embrace its longstanding African-American members and remains conflicted about the meaning of full inclusion of gays and lesbians, it is being awakened to the reality of an ever-widening spectrum of ethnic and cultural diversity. Hispanic, First Nation, and Asian-American populations are growing at faster rates than other groups. This means that the future growth and relevance of the Episcopal Church will be strongly linked to its ability to perceive and accept the changed cultural and ethnic context in

which it exists. Will the church have the will and leadership capacity to translate these changing demographics
into meaning that gives an urgency to change our
behavior? Will the church finally be able to elevate diversity to a deep level of mission integration that takes
members beyond any specific training program to a movement of true transformation of beliefs and practices?

A SHIFT IN SIZE

The second significant change that will have an impact on
the church is the slight yet steady decline in growth and in
giving. Half of the congregations in the United States have
fewer than 100 active members; 25 percent have fewer
than 50 regularly participating adults.[3] Of the 7,145
congregations in the Episcopal Church, slightly more than
half of the churches have between one and 75 members.
These family-size parishes account for 17.6 percent of the
average Sunday attendance in the Episcopal Church. This
level of attendance is slightly higher than the 16.3 percent
average Sunday attendance of the 205 resource-size
congregations. These statistics support those who say that
the Episcopal Church is "a church of small churches." But
nearly half of Episcopalians are members of resource-size
parishes, and this accounts for the truth of those who say
that the Episcopal Church is "a denomination of large
churches." It is both/and; we live with the paradox that we
are both small and large, which makes the debate over size
irrelevant according to the Reverend Canon Keith Brown,
author of "Some Key Data and Trends in the Episcopal
Church."[4] Canon Brown says that both small and large
congregations are facing declining plate and pledge
revenue and rising operational and maintenance costs.
The predominately small, rural, non-endowed, urban
parishes and ministries will be more quickly affected by
these dips and drops because they often lack the people
resources and financial cushion that many larger parishes

have. An increasing number of the smaller parishes will be unable to support full-time clergy or to provide adequate compensation or sufficient health insurance coverage for their staff.

In addition to the decline in church membership and attendance, the lower percentage increases in giving in Episcopal churches are indicative of a potentially precarious situation facing the church. These changes, while mirroring national statistics and trends for other mainline Protestant denominations, are too disturbing to be quickly dismissed.

A SHIFT IN NUMBER OF LEADERS

A third wave of change that will affect the Episcopal Church in the future is the numerical decline of ordained leaders and the anticipated turnover of leadership in every order. The degree of change in leadership in five of the eight Episcopal provinces in the United States is significant, as seen in the table below.

DECLINE IN NUMBERS OF EPISCOPAL CLERGY BY PROVINCE

PROVINCE	PERCENT OF CHANGE FROM 1972–2002	PERCENT OF CHANGE FROM 1972–2007
I	– 7.9	– 716.6
II	– 21	– 724.4
III	– 1.4	– 77.3
IV	16.5	9.2
V	– 20.2	– 728.8
VI	– 16.1	– 722.3
VII	4.5	2.9
VIII	0.6	– 74.4
Total	– 4.4	– 710.4

Adapted from "Church Trends and Policy Institutions,"
a report of the Church Pension Group by Matthew Price (July 17, 2007)

In addition to this decline in the number of ordained clergy, a significant number of bishops are retiring over the next decade: According to statistics compiled by the Church Pension Fund, a total of seventy-four bishops will be eligible to retire in the next ten years. Leadership transitions will occur at diocesan, provincial, and national levels as well. While no scientific studies have been undertaken to tell us the degree of shift in lay leadership, observation and experience indicate that the church will face significant transition here also. The rates of leadership attrition and turnover will be felt even more keenly because of the changes previously noted.

There are other statistics pointing to troubling trends: of the 1,221 clergy enrolled in the Church Pension Fund, 23.6 percent are thirty-four or younger. About a third are fifty-five or older. The percentage of female clergy in the fifty-four and younger age ranges is declining. At the same time, although the Episcopal Church has seen declines in church school attendance, number of baptisms, and number of members, the number of clergy has been increasing. The increasing enrollment and declining average age of seminarians offers hope for the future, but also raises the key question of how to best prepare them to lead. This younger generation of leaders is facing a very challenging time and a changing church. How are they being prepared to deal with these adaptive challenges? How is their curriculum and education changing to equip them to lead in the midst of chronic change and to resolve the conflicts that accompany it? There are no clear, consistent, comforting answers to date.

The three shifts, or "waves of change," and the larger context referred to earlier point to the need for a different practice of leadership. While the inclusion and meaningful involvement of a younger generation of ordained ministers is a highly desirable goal and gives some assurances that the church may be able to replenish parish and diocesan vacancies, the absence of notable programs for leadership formation and development that are attuned to understanding these larger shifts is indicative of a pending leadership crisis.

In the late 1970s and 1980s the Diocese of Indianapolis was one of a number of Episcopal dioceses that provided programs for seminary graduates called "Training in Ministry." These graduates were placed in parishes for one year, where they received intensive coaching, mentoring, and educational experiences that prepared them for the reality of the priesthood. This one-year period permitted them opportunities to learn more about congregational dynamics and culture, to explore the roles and responsibilities required of ordained leaders, and to practice carrying out ministry. When they left to assume parish responsibilities, they felt they were well prepared, since there was not as much of a gap between their cognitive understanding and the reality of parish life. Without such intentional preparation, the gap is widening and the number of failed ministries is increasing.

The gap between the challenges we face and the church's acknowledgment of and capacity to address them will widen unless there are intentional and well thought-out responses. We need imaginative initiatives comparable in boldness to those initiated in previous decades when the church found itself being moved to the margins. Transformational change begins with an accurate reading of reality, one of the attributes of the new leadership sorely needed.

---

reading reality truthfully

Reading reality truthfully is no easy feat. Research shows that this is particularly true for religious leaders. The 2000 Faith Communities Today (FACT) survey of 726

Episcopal congregations out of 1100 randomly selected parishes revealed that only a few of the church leaders surveyed were willing to admit to any substantial congregational decline. Although 40 percent of them experienced 10 percent or more decline, only 105 accurately reported this level of decline. Even these 105 leaders reported 10 to 20 percent *higher levels of increases* in congregational participation and stability than were factually true. Because of this tendency to under-represent facts and deny reality, researchers used the parochial reports to obtain more accurate data.

How seriously will the church take the signs of potential decline?

In true Anglican style, there is a question of the veracity of the FACT study's findings because of inconsistency in criteria used in the past to collect and report data. Parochial reports may not be exactly accurate, since much of the data is subjectively gathered. In his online essay "Is the Episcopal Church Growing (or Declining)?" Kirk Hadaway cautions against drawing absolute conclusions from the data because of the inconsistencies.[5] In research conducted by Matthew Price, Vice President of Analytical Research at the Church Pension Group, findings show that the pattern of decline in membership and attendance in the Episcopal Church is less than the other mainstream denominations.[6] Perhaps the reading of reality means examining the data from multiple perspectives. Doing so can lead to increased understanding of what is true, and a better sense of how to use this understanding to engage in responsible action.

Those who say that the church is in a period of decline are often dismissed as doomsayers intent on portraying the Episcopal Church in a negative light. Those who deny decline respond by pointing to examples of impressive growth as if they were normative examples rather than exceptions. There are Episcopal churches that have grown stronger and larger in the past decade; there are examples of parishes where the sweeping societal shifts and adverse demographic trends have not been deterrents to their health or vitality. It is inspiring to point out the exemplary—and also wise to revisit the data reflecting decline, and discern what it means. A decline of 8,201 members in the Episcopal Church in 2002 averaged out as a loss of only 1.1 members per church. While the average is too low to be noticed in any single congregational context, in aggregate form this degree of decline is a problematic sign. When the statistics are translated across the denomination, the rate of growth is equal to the rate of loss. The Episcopal Church is in a plateau at best. Hadaway writes, "Clearly we need more vibrant healthy churches, but growing as a denomination will require systemic changes."

What will we do to develop and prepare new leaders differently for a different time?

Given the information collected to date by reputable sources within and outside of the Episcopal Church, it would be irresponsible to ignore or minimize the signs of erosion and demise. Refusing to pay attention to them reinforces a climate of denial and defensiveness, and will ultimately lead to the church being ill prepared to deal with the future impact of the shifts we are experiencing today.

In examining the significant shifts facing the church, we know that what were once unquestioned assumptions and commonly shared beliefs are now being vigorously challenged and debated. The integration and application of scientific knowledge with sacred beliefs and faith practices is as challenging as it was in the time of Copernicus. What has been taught as religious and biblical truth is frequently perceived as being at odds with scientific knowledge. Responding responsibly is made all the more difficult by the fact that we are in a time in which leaders lack the tools and resources that can be used to manage effectively the tension and anxiety that accompanies these systemic changes. The gap between where the church is and where we want it to be is a place of no longer and not yet, a place where change and confusion can overshadow enlightenment and clarity.

While the reading of reality that emphasizes "what is right with the church" can ignite a sense of hope and optimism, the reading of reality that identifies erosion of attendance and giving cannot be ignored. A one-sided view is insufficient to address the long-term, deep, systemic, and transformational changes needed in the church. The effect that the adverse statistics and trends cited will ultimately have on the church is dependent on the kind of leadership we exercise. What the church needs most now is courageous and honest leadership—moral and ethical leaders who will, as Craig Dykstra reminds us, "read reality truthfully so that they can respond responsibly."

It is essential for leaders to sit with and discuss the data collected by and for the church, no matter how voluminous and contradictory it may be, if we are to understand what it means and know how best to respond. A deeper and more insightful reading of the information will enable the church to discover what it needs to retain as precious and what it needs to let go. In this process it will discover the need for a new form of leadership and can sow the seeds of its future transformation. We are reminded in John's gospel of what can result when we are able to let go: "Unless a grain of wheat falls into earth and dies, it remains just a single grain; but if it dies, it bears much fruit" (John 12:24). The time of no longer and not yet is a time of dying to an old order so the new one can be born. In this gap between what is and what can be is an opportunity for change that can be transformational.

North United Methodist Church (NUMC) in Indianapolis, Indiana, is nearly ninety years old. The church was started before the Great Depression by a Methodist bishop "who had a heart for urban ministry," and is at the intersection of two main arteries, Meridian Street and 38th Street. It is located at the center of four neighborhoods—Meridian Kessler, Butler Tarkington, Mapleton Fall Creek, and the United Northwest Neighborhood Association. NUMC began as a small Methodist Episcopal church and did not build its first building until the members had the money required. This strong sense of fiscal responsibility and social justice remains today, as the pastor, the Reverend Kevin Armstrong, leads that congregation in looking at more ways to invest economically in the surrounding area.

The congregation has opened its doors to a diverse population and currently has one thousand members who attend two Sunday services. There is a high commitment to Christian education for adults throughout the week. About 70 percent of the members participate in these educational formation offerings.

In the six years of his ministry there, Kevin states that the greatest challenge he has faced is dealing with change and the nature of change, in spite of the fact that "change is in the DNA" of the church. Kevin returned to NUMC in 2002 as a staff member for three years before becoming the chief pastor. He had previously served NUMC as Minister of Community Ministry fifteen years ago and left to be the pastor of a downtown Methodist church for nine years. He returned because of the church's "commitment to the city and its theological bent." Kevin led a change from what he describes as an outdated institutional structure to a leaner, more theologically grounded form of team ministry. Multiple committees were eliminated and replaced with teams that reflect the vocational identity of the church—equipping all of its members for leadership and ministry. The church successfully raised the funds to build its new Fellowship Center. The change was difficult, in part because Kevin feels he could have communicated the process of change in more helpful ways. But he began by asking a key question: "How do we equip *all* of our leaders in the congregation?" The result has been the involvement of more of its members in neighborhood ministries.

Kevin says that what helped him most was strong lay involvement, good friendships, reliance on God, and a personal sabbath he keeps every Friday with his wife. He works closely with an administrative staff team, and has a spiritual director and an executive coach whom he sees once a month. He has learned the importance of self-care and self-reflection in leadership. This grounded him through his leadership of significant internal change and continues to sustain him as he leads the church into its next phase of responding to external community needs and continued economic development of the area.

Kevin has no label for the way he leads; he learned through observing and listening and asking a question that launched a new way of ministering. He describes his primary roles as storyteller and meaning-maker in the church. His leadership is grounded in a theology that understands mission as the chief reason for the existence of the church and the preparation of leaders for outreach in the community as the chief expression of it. Kevin created the hospitable yet challenging space in which the congregation could struggle with how it ministered to its members and to the larger community. He waited patiently for the right time and the right way to respond. The rich history of stewardship and outreach he found at NUMC needed new forms of expression in order to remain relevant and effective in the current context. As strong as the church was, Kevin saw the need to make it stronger and better able to deal with the complexity of contemporary change. The process of reading reality truthfully helped him to transform the members and their ministries. And as a result, the surrounding community and residents are the beneficiaries. This is an example of transforming leadership and how it can significantly respond responsibly to change.

———

The question that began this chapter—*"Can you help us?"*—continues to haunt me. It demands more time and attention, and the answer is inextricably linked to leadership, which only prolongs the ability to respond. The capacity to inspire and lead change that is transformational comes from a depth of understanding of self and systems and a depth of faith and belief that enables the leader to face adversity without fear—the fear that cripples creativity and imagination and erodes the courage to persist in doing what is right. Transforming leadership has this depth. It *can* be acquired, but not without an examination of the shifting paradigms that lead to redefining leadership. And so it is to those paradigms that we turn next.

chapter two

Shifting Paradigms

The responsible action is like a statement in dialogue
considerate of the previous statement and made in
anticipation of reply; it looks forward as well as backward.
　　　　　　　　　　　　　　　—H. Richard Niebuhr

A New Yorker magazine cartoon in which Charles
Dickens and his London publisher are meeting
captures humorously the desire for certainty in a time of
great change. The publisher, while holding a huge manu-
script in his hands and peering over his thin, narrow
reading glasses with an expression of deep consternation
on his face, says, "Look, Mr. Dickens, it's either the best
of times or the worst of times, but it can't be both!"

Well, it can be and *is* a both/and period of history in
which the gap between current reality and a preferred
future seems distressingly wide. Many congregations
desire respite from what feels like a chronic in-between
state of siege, in which such major issues as urban exodus,
changing demographics, declining contributions, budget
shortfalls, same-gender blessings/marriage, and membership losses demand attention. Some want immediate resolution; others welcome prioritization; still others yearn for

a past time of familiarity; and more vocal advocates believe a return to mission is the solution to the angst. The anxiety that can so easily flourish in a time of no longer and not yet puts considerable pressure on leaders to do something—anything—to relieve the discomfort. Those who react without taking adequate time to think about the emotions that lie beneath these demands will be seriously limited in how effective they will be in helping congregants to respond in faith rather than in fear. In prematurely alleviating the ambiguity, the leader colludes with congregants to avoid the chaos and confusion out of which a true new beginning can come. Leading in the gap, especially in a culture so prideful of quick fixes and immediate responses, is challenging and difficult work.

The space that ethical leadership creates is one of respect, dignity, openness, and trust—the kind that inspires others to claim their voices and name their truths. —*Katherine Tyler Scott*

Ambiguity is inevitable in times of significant cultural shift, and in no other emotional state are we more exposed to the reality that two profound and seemingly incompatible truths can coexist. We are reminded that sheer intellectual ability and unrelenting persistence in problem-solving are not sufficient in dealing with this paradox. More than these qualities are needed to figure out what is right action. Learning to hold the tension of the opposites together long enough to understand what is right action requires time to reflect and silent space to be and to hear the inner wisdom. Out of this space true dialogue can begin, and multiple options can be created to deal with seemingly intractable problems. The potential to offer this hospitable space to experience grace and wisdom resides within the Episcopal Church.

The faith tradition of the Episcopal Church once served to equip its members with a greater capacity to deal with paradox—a gift it needs to recover for its own sake and that of the world. If the church can help its members reclaim this gift, its members will be better equipped to navigate the current terrain of complex change without disabling fear and clinging to old behaviors that cannot work. Reclaiming this gift will be transformational itself because doing so requires practicing a different kind of leadership, leadership consciously and deeply rooted in the knowledge and belief that we are the result and the recipients of an eternal, enduring Love. It is this Love that gives us the courage to stand in the gap, to be in a both/and reality, to hold the tension of the opposites together, and to have the courage to take right action. It is this Love that provides the capacity to lead others to a deeper understanding of events and issues in their lives. It is this Love that seeds the belief in something greater than ego and self-interest. And it is this Love-drenched leadership that enables diverse communities to respond from a core of coherence and strength to the turbulence and trouble in the world. In essence, the leadership most needed now is profoundly spiritual.

According to Jeffery Sheller, author of "Faith in America," the United States remains the most religious and diverse of western democracies.[1] A religious structure of some kind exists for every 865 people in the country. Eighty percent of Americans say that they have experienced the presence of God or a spiritual force. A deep spiritual hunger exists in the public sphere; individuals and institutions are responding to it using language and practices borrowed from—but not always acknowledged as being from—the church. Bible study groups have sprung up in workplaces; poetry and prayer are part of executive trainings; independent groups meet seeking vocational discernment, meaning, and community. Televangelists and talk show hosts attract millions of viewers when discussing ways to live a more authentic and meaningful life. There is a growing spiritual hunger and a desire to learn about the Divine. When the church recognizes and responds to this hunger, it becomes stronger. The FACT study shows that those congregations that are rated the highest in vitality are also the strongest in spiritual and educational offerings such as retreats, study circles, and prayer groups. Paying attention to spiritual needs leads to a congregation that is well-equipped to exercise ministry.

The very charism that once distinctly defined the Episcopal Church is precisely what so many people are seeking: the ability to embrace uncertainty and ambiguity responsibly. In other words, the spiritual search is for the development of character, the identification of calling, the alignment between belief and behavior, and the opportunity to make a significant contribution to the world. Character, calling, congruence, and contribution—these are the elements of an authentic Christian life and what congregational leaders must manifest themselves and elicit in others. The yearning and search for meaning and significance reflect the need for a changing paradigm of leadership, a paradigm that recognizes the spiritual nature of leadership.

the scientific paradigm of reality

The current reading of reality demands an examination of the Scientific Age paradigm and an evaluation of the viability of a seventeenth-century view in a twenty-first-century world. This paradigm is shaped by a belief in the primacy of science, a primacy that has greatly contributed to significant scientific progress and amazing technological advancements. It is a view that has influenced the ways in which the majority of institutions are structured, managed, and led; and in many cases it has dominated the cultures of business, politics, government, and religion.

This paradigm reflects the core values and beliefs espoused in the larger culture—individual responsibility, initiative, autonomy, and independence, and a top-down leadership style. It worships data and technical skills, denies loss, and depends on command-and-control leadership.

THE DIVINATION OF DATA

In the scientific paradigm facts are not only highly valued, they are perceived as the sole reality and the primary arbiters of truth. What cannot be measured or scientifically proven is often devalued and dismissed. This change emerged in the Age of Reason, when religion was relegated to the realm of unproved fact, and perceived with doubt and distrust. Non-scientific data was suspect as a source of veracity; objectivity became the trusted determinant of truth. The vestiges of this view can be seen in the church when facts are so prized they become more important than imagination or faith.

The deification of facts can sometimes be seen in the ways religious organizations handle financial matters. Financial stewardship and fiscal prudence are important, but if they are allowed to dominate decisions concerning the mission of the parish, the core of why the congregation exists—mission—becomes tainted. For example, if a parish or diocesan treasurer becomes the chief architect and decision-maker of how the church's funds are to be spent, or when the bottom line for being able to entertain or implement innovative ideas becomes that of the bank balance, we are likely observing a church culture in which facts are dominant, not faith. Reliance on faith in making mission decisions should not be an excuse for financial irresponsibility, but if mission is not a major consideration in decision-making, the church operates like any secular operation, but with a religious façade. The right leadership can ensure both fiscal responsibility *and* fidelity to mission. Finances need to serve the mission rather than the mission serving finances. Character, calling, and congruence lead to contributions of commitment and monetary resources.

Because facts are so highly valued in the Scientific Age paradigm, data is seen as an essential resource. The collection and acquisition of data *is* important, and is used to advance change and growth in the church. In many instances successful stewardship and capital campaigns are data-driven. So a reliance on data can be very constructive in the church, but when data is used to rank, judge, or value members, it does not serve a community of faith well. When the focus of data-gathering and analysis is a common, shared vision, and those with differing gifts are helped to see how what they have to offer is equally valued, the whole community is enriched and strengthened.

If one member suffers, all suffer together with it; if one member is honored, all rejoice together with it. *(1 Corinthians 12:26)*

Furthermore, when data-gathering and analysis focuses on the current, immediate, in-the-moment understanding of issues so common in the scientific paradigm, the "wide span of awareness" that leadership requires is frequently missing. When a longer view exists, leaders can better see the complexities as well as the possibilities of change, and they can impart this broader perspective to others. A wider view enables a community to feel a sense of identity, of cultural coherence and belonging, while also seeing that the body of Christ exists to serve a much larger world than just that inside the church walls. When the ability to see a larger context does not exist, the capacity for creating a healthy, outward-looking congregational culture is diminished.

I have often heard congregational leaders who are in the process of calling a rector emphatically say they want their choice to be someone who will serve their parish and be more available to the members. They make no allowance for the leader to be involved in diocesan, provincial, or national church committees. Such a parochial view undermines the relationship parishes have with the whole church. and the responsibility they have to develop leaders for it.

TECHNICAL VERSUS ADAPTIVE SKILLS
The adaptive challenges of our time cannot be addressed effectively with a paradigm predicated on perceiving problems as technical and the skills needed to solve them as mechanistic. Specific competencies and concrete, prescribed steps with tasks that can be predictably applied to a problem in order to find a clear solution are highly prized in the scientific paradigm. Examples of such skills in a church would be repair and maintenance of equipment, printing service leaflets and the parish annual report, preparing the altar for worship, designating parking, and so on.

A technical view of our current problems will produce inadequate solutions. Such views reinforce either/or thinking and leave the fault lines of race, gender, and class—places of division—untouched. When people are objectified and treated in ways that diminish their dignity and worth, the entire community suffers. Such behavior severs the Christian community from the source of its true identity and power—the knowledge that we are all unconditionally loved and valued. As Paul reminds us, the body of Christ consists of many members, and every part is connected and valued.

Congregations that depend on technical fixes for adaptive problems can forget that the Spirit of the Divine exists in everything and in everyone. In *To Know As We Are Known,* Parker Palmer writes of the functional atheism that results when this spiritual wisdom is lacking: "The knower now stands like a master builder in the midst of chaos, trying to fashion a world fit for habitation. Now we alone are the creators; with our facts we make reality."[2]

An example of leaders making their own reality with facts and treating them as the sole reality occurred at an annual meeting in a large urban parish. The parish treasurer gave the year-end financial report in an impressive, colorful PowerPoint presentation. The graphs and pie charts showed a three-year decline in membership and in giving. The rector's public response to the report was nevertheless upbeat. He said that the parish had raised more money than it had in any previous year, and ended by proclaiming the stewardship campaign a huge success. The knowledge that the reason for this was that fewer members were giving more was not noted, and neither was the downward trend in fundraising. It was a "master builder moment," with the leader standing in the midst of chaos, "trying to fashion a world fit for habitation"—he alone was the creator of reality.

Later the rector and the parish administrator both refuted an observation by a parishioner that the outreach budget had in fact been reduced by half. The budget showed a figure that at first glance appeared to be the same as the previous year's figure. In reality, the previous budget had been cut in half before the year-end and the commitments made by the Outreach Committee in the past year had been rolled over into the budget presented. So the budget was indeed half of what it had been the previous year. "Facts" had been used to distort the truth, and to portray a preferred rather than an actual reality. Trust, which is so essential to healthy congregations and one of the clear indicators of spiritually grounded leadership, became a casualty in this transaction.

In the Scientific Age paradigm organizations are viewed mechanistically; the structures and those inhabiting them are viewed as separate, interchangeable, and replaceable parts. The operating belief is that if one part breaks down it can be immediately replaced with minimal effect on the system's overall performance, productivity, and profitability. The Management by Objectives (MBO) craze that swept through the Episcopal Church in the 1970s is an example of the mechanistic view. Churches certainly need to operate more efficiently and effectively, but they are not businesses where the capital is money and product, not mission and people.

> Good leadership doesn't come out of technique. It comes out of the individual's ongoing journey of spiritual formation, of clarifying one's own heart, of finding the ground on which they stand."
> — *Parker Palmer*

   This approach is still resident today in the form of an obsession with strategic planning. One very prominent parish adopted this corporate model. When applied to the parish, the planning process ignored the organic and spiritual nature of the culture and its reliance on human beings as its "capital." Members were treated as if they were movable widgets in a system of rigid lines of authority and accountability. After a year of this planning process, the end product was an elaborate array of goals, objectives, strategies, and tasks detached from any understanding of institutional history, ecclesiology, theology, or spiritual vision. In the end most people in the congregation expressed feelings of being "worn down." Few possessed a clear vision of the non-technical qualities that define a church community—caring relationships, involvement, ownership, love, and spirit—all of which had been desecrated by the rigidity of the process and its ignorance of the culture. There was little energy or inspiration left to achieve what many had labored so long to produce.

DENIAL OF LOSS

Another example of the Scientific Age paradigm operating in congregations is the response of the church to loss and decline. When the immediate response to these events is to deny or minimize them, then the church is operating as if it were engaged in "spin." A mechanistic mindset is in operation when members leave a parish and their leaving is ignored and the impact on a congregation is denied.

A number of clergy and lay leaders with whom I have spoken have expressed a "good riddance" attitude toward congregants who have left their parishes over unresolved conflict. They immediately turn their attention to "mission," and to recruiting new members. Those members left behind handle these losses in a variety of ways. Some agree with the good riddance posture, a few feel empathy with those who left, but most are silent. Clergy interpret their silence as consent when it likely means much more. For many, beneath the silence is a layer of brokenness and grief, sadness and helplessness, a disconnect between what is preached and what is being practiced.

The climate created by a mechanistic handling of loss makes it impossible for the congregation to mourn and to explore the meaning and impact of these leavings on the community that remains. Clergy who convey a message of "good riddance" without dealing with the spectrum of the effect the losses have on a congregation prevent those left behind from truly moving on. Leaders who respond in this manner to member losses create a climate in which congregants question their own value to the community. The aborted grief process sets up a culture in which it becomes easy to scapegoat, to split individuals and groups into side-taking factions, and to repress normal feelings of anger and sadness.

There are some hopeful examples in which a more relational paradigm can shape the response to member loss. In this paradigm, leaders do not just focus on those leaving because of unresolved conflict: *all* leavings are noticed, and the message is that *all* members of the community matter. Clergy meet with those who have decided to leave, and the parish lists the names of those leaving in the bulletin and newsletter, states where they are going, and offers good wishes to them. Some parishes acknowledge imminent departures of long-term members during the worship service, permitting them and the congregation to say their goodbyes face-to-face. Such practices are reassuring and enlivening to those remaining behind. The clergy become the embodiment of the gospel and the teachings of Jesus; those leaving and those left behind hear the message that God loves them. The congregation has an opportunity to tell those who are leaving that they will be remembered and missed by the community. Leaders can reassure the congregation that change is a normal part of a community's life, that this parish can handle the ebb and flow that accompanies change: *We are strong and we will continue to grow in service and in love.* This approach differs vastly from that evoked by the Scientific Age paradigm, in which the end goal of achieving increased numbers outweighs the mission of developing a truly religious community. The statistics in the parochial reports matter, just as the quality of the relationships between the people in the community matter.

DYNAMICS OF LEADERSHIP:
COMMAND AND CONTROL
The top-down leadership in the Scientific Age paradigm is typically expressed in a command-and-control style. It is equated with title, status, and formal position. There is an automatic acknowledgment that the individual's formal role carries a certain level of authority and power that is recognized by the system. The formal leader exercises this

power by virtue of title not just because of character or the respect of followers.

When top-down leaders are confronted with a lack of consensus in the group they pull rank. The importance of such authority is evident when a congregation defers to it in internal disagreements and conflicts. Deference (or capitulation) can be heard in statements like, "Tell us what to do—after all, you are the rector!" The message is clear: the priest is being accorded ultimate power. But deferred or canonical authority is not leadership, and unless there is a crisis in which the top-down style is the appropriate way to intervene, it is an unhealthy exercise of power accompanied by a lack of responsible followership.

Clergy whose primary style of operating is top-down and coercive survive only because the parishioners collude with and reinforce this style. An example of this collusion is parishioners who absolve themselves of personal responsibility by reinforcing that the clergy are "in charge," or the congregation involved in a clergy search that puts the real work on hold "until the rector is called." The reluctance or refusal to accept personal responsibility and the legitimate authority that comes from the ministry of all the baptized perpetuates the autocratic behavior of clergy and leads to a weak and unhealthy culture. When clergy accept the projection of being totally responsible and in sole control, learned helplessness is being taught to congregants. Each time a problem occurs in which members of the congregation absolve themselves of legitimate and responsible authority and leadership, they are teaching themselves a form of powerlessness. Few groups exhibiting this behavior will consciously choose to give up their dependency and the comfort of the familiar in order to become more responsible. To do so would usher in a period of anxiety and dis-ease, a time of being unsettled and challenged. While the long-term reward for taking this risk is the evolution of a healthier congregation, the desire for relief in the short-term often prevents this. Unless there is a strong, self-differentiated leader who is able to give the congregation back its real work and baptismal authority, it will be unable to take the necessary risks to change and grow.

Signs of healthy spiritual leadership can be seen in the kind of interdependency between the rector and the congregation that creates generosity, freedom, creativity, and hospitality to strangers. It can be seen in the relationships that enable the community to see and reach outside and beyond itself. Such leaders help the congregation to tackle difficult issues in substantive rather than superficial ways, and inspire it to question familiar ways of knowing, to embrace change, and truly to value differences and diversity. These leaders have the courage to examine their inner and outer sources of power, and are able to own and examine them and their impact on the church. They can evaluate how their power is perceived, authorized, and exercised, and how and to whom they delegate it. The issues related to power and authority in congregational life are rarely directly confronted until or unless there is a crisis, such as a financial shortfall, a moral failing of the clergy or key staff member, or the retirement or death of the priest. Congregations are rendered bereft and left in a state of panic and reactivity when a crisis forces them to assume responsibility they have not learned to exercise in the past, but have given solely to clergy.

Highly dependent congregations in major transition or crisis are typically in denial and defensive; they prefer to look externally for the causes of their problems rather than within themselves. If this reactivity continues, they will be unable to claim the power within the community to change this destructive cycle. To break out of it requires adopting a different paradigm, one that understands that some problems can only be resolved by letting go of fear, surrendering one's ego to God, being reflective and receptive, becoming vulnerable, and struggling with the tough questions about the state of trust, relationship, and communication with one another.

The challenge presented in the Scientific Age paradigm is that power is perceived as finite and only a few can have it. The leader is at the top, with a few individuals directly beneath. Those providing support and maintenance functions are at the bottom, and the majority of members are in between the top and the bottom of this pyramid. Competition for a higher position and status is heightened in the system because of the perception that there is a finite reservoir of power. The measure of success and worth in this paradigm is how high (and fast) one can rise, further increasing the degree of competition. Humorous stories abound about church staff and congregants (choir directors, altar guild members, treasurers) who work competitively rather than collaboratively. This is always an indication of a belief that power is limited in the system, and with only so much to go around, everyone or everybody in the system has to protect what they have and not let it be diminished. In fact, they must work harder to acquire more or what little they have will be of less value. Perhaps a past history of competent performance, longstanding dedication, and loyalty helped them amass considerable power, but there is a sense of having to be on constant guard to retain it. Holding on to power tightly closes off opportunities to look creatively at the challenges the church faces. It prevents the church from asking the difficult questions.

♦ What can the church learn from the past that will enable it to strengthen its financial health and change a downward trend in growth and giving?

♦ What will need to change in the content, teaching methodology, and preparation of the next generation in order for this group to effectively occupy the leadership positions that will be open in the near future?

◆ How will the next generation of leaders be best prepared to assume the governance and leadership responsibilities essential to the survival and future vitality of the Episcopal Church?

◆ What will the operating paradigm for congregational life and leadership need to be, in order to have a spiritually strong and healthy parish?

The struggle to respond to questions such as these is integral to the process of transformation.

Those who perceive that the Episcopal Church is in crisis are correct—the crisis is one of leadership. Several groups and institutions recognize this and are attempting to respond. Some Episcopal seminaries—Seabury, Virginia, General—have adopted missions that explicitly express their development of leadership using a different paradigm of ministry. The Seabury experiment offers an entirely new view of the role of a seminary and how it needs to prepare clergy and lay leaders. The Office of Pastoral Care and Ministry at the Episcopal Church Center has likewise revised its training program for newly consecrated bishops, and added substantive content, greater depth, and year-long coaching support for participants. The General Convention's revision of the Title III canons concerning leadership in ministry acknowledges places of discernment other than a parish. Clergy renewal and clergy wellness programs, such as those offered by the Lilly Endowment, tell us that the caliber of leadership in the congregation and diocese affects the health and well-being of the whole church. Claude Payne, retired bishop of Texas, has begun an initiative called "The Gathering of Leaders." This group brings together clergy and bishops from all across the country to work on enhancing their sense of call, mission, and ministry in order to transform the Episcopal Church. These meetings occur one to two times a year, and to date have reached 144 clergy. Bishop Payne sees the continuing spiritual and theological formation of existing clergy as critical to the future health of the church. These and other such responses go to the very heart and soul of the Episcopal Church, and ultimately, to its sustainability and survival.

To confront the reality and achieve these goals, the church needs to adopt a different paradigm of leadership, one that reflects a deep understanding of contextual realities, seriously values an interdependent community, and embraces the spiritual nature of leadership.

---

the emergence of a new paradigm

Western culture has long held two conflicting views of reality—one scientific and the other spiritual. The scientific paradigm has been the dominant view of reality over the previous two centuries; it discounted or minimized the spiritual. Religious institutions generally ignored or marginalized scientific research that challenged their beliefs and views. The resistance to learning from either of these two realms has contributed to the irrelevance of theological explanations of issues and events. In the public sphere it encouraged the portrayal of the church as a closed society, not as a community engaged in inclusiveness, learning, formation, and truth-seeking. The long-standing divisions between science and religion and the compartmentalization of data have allowed potentially constructive contributions of science to be misused, such as the categorization and classification of people in ways that are dehumanizing. Yet when these two realms are brought together and their leaders engage in dialogue, transformation can take place.

The once common view of the universe as a collection of separate, disconnected, and competing parts is changing to the view of a system of interconnected parts, each moving in relationship to one another. The old Newtonian understanding of the universe has been shattered by the knowledge of quantum physics. We now know that the earth is composed of infinitesimal particles moving at speeds faster than light in fields of energy. We are part of a vast system of visible and invisible networks so interconnected that a change in one part affects the whole. This knowledge has affected our perception of the nature of the universe and changed our view of reality. The two characteristics so definitive of the Scientific Age paradigm—dualism and hierarchy—are changing. The emerging paradigm is one of relationship and the changes it brings are dramatic. The impact on how we define and perceive leadership, and how we view and structure organizations, is profound. We now need different skills and processes for sharing and integrating information, different methods for influencing others, and different ways of making meaning and forming leaders.

> We are entering a time when the primary leadership challenges will not be technical, but transformational. It is a time when leaders will fail, not because of a lack of strategy or resources, but from a failure of imagination. —*Michael Jones*

The massive amount of data from multiple disciplines, and the challenge of discerning what it all means, while striving to behave with integrity and veracity, demands a level of integration in leadership that is unfamiliar and not easily or quickly acquired. Unlike technical skills that can be applied exceptionally well in situations where an issue or problem is clearly defined and the response or solution is quickly evident, the Relationship Age paradigm requires adaptive skills. Adaptive skills are effective when the problems are not clear and the responses to them are not evident, such as the eradication of poverty, developing and sustaining ecumenical dialogue, organizing and sustaining peace, encouraging reconciliation between opposing groups or individuals, developing theological education resources, determining how a diocese will respond to General Convention resolutions, reducing budget deficits, and other concerns. The new paradigm is organic, believes in a model of shared power and authority, and involves inner work and self-differentiation.

ORGANIC LEADERSHIP
One of the hallmarks of leadership in the Relationship Age is the recognition that those who have the problems must be engaged in solving them. Unlike the top-down structure of leadership found in the Scientific Age paradigm, leadership in the Relationship Age paradigm is circular and organic. It exists in multiple places and is widely distributed. The leaders may not be immediately visible; they are, as Parker Palmer reminds us, "hidden in plain sight." These are individuals who may or may not have a formal title or status; they may lack the familiar external credentialing usually conferred on those we label "leader." These individuals are recognized as possessing gifts that positively contribute to the improvement of a whole community. The differences in their gifts are recognized and equally valued. Individuals are accorded value not solely because of title or status but because of their character, calling, congruence, and the value of their contribution to the whole.

Facts in this paradigm are valued, but they are not viewed as the sole reality or demigods of truth. They are perceived and treated as another way of knowing, another determinant of truth. Equally important as *having* facts is figuring out what they *mean,* and how to translate and integrate them in the day-to-day ministries of the church.

Theologian and historian Fredrica Harris Thompsett has commented, "With so much going on in our society and world, *what* we choose to notice reveals *who* we are."[3] The way we deal with facts is an expression of identity. We are deluged with data; we have an incalculable collection of facts. What we do with them, what we choose to pay attention to, and how we interpret and make meaning of these facts is a process that is integral to transformational leadership.

During an adult education forum in my home parish, a large and vital midwestern urban congregation, the presenter began a discussion about prayer and action. After a period of quiet reflection one parishioner recounted how she and another member had attended a seminar on greenhouse gas pollution a few weeks before. Both had some awareness of a serious pollution problem from media coverage, but neither had many facts. They learned that the United States was responsible for the emission of nearly 70 percent of the carbon dioxide in the world and that the countries with the lowest emission rates were being hurt the most by these emissions. For the first time the facts had new significance. The data had been translated into a meaningful and compelling tale of economic and social injustice. The creation of meaning helped them to see clearly the schism between a profession of belief and the incongruent actions. The reframing of the problem of greenhouse gas emissions led to a parish-wide "green project" and the education of members about the many small ways they could help reverse the environmental and human devastation taking place.

The Relationship Age paradigm is an organic network of relationships and shared responsibility in service to something transcendent of ego and of narrow self-interests. The theological and liturgical life of the Episcopal Church reflects this paradigm whenever the faith community gathers to remember and to give praise and thanksgiving during the Eucharist. Each time we partake of the Body and Blood of Christ, we are being reminded that the mission of the church is "to restore all people to unity with God and each other in Christ" (BCP 855). The restoration of unity is the development of community and relationship.

SHARED POWER AND AUTHORITY

In this paradigm, positional authority is recognized as power, but unlike the Scientific Age paradigm, power is not the equivalent of leadership. To meet the definition of leadership, power must be tempered with a heavy infusion of altruism—the capacity to care for another human being, to feed the poor and care for those on the margins of society. Altruism and authority are inextricably linked; the exercise of power merges with compassion and empathy. This convergence is the catalyst for real transformation of culture and leadership.

Authority to lead is internal and external. It also comes from followers. The power to lead is generated by letting it go and sharing it with others. Sharing power creates abundance rather than scarcity. It is generative because it is exercised *with* others rather than *over* others. The more power is shared, the more power is created. The power invested in a leader is returned tenfold to the group and enables its members to claim their own power to lead. The leader is the "first among equals" in the Relationship Age paradigm, and creates the space for the practice of generosity and a spirit of abundance to prevail.

Instead of the dichotomous thinking so prevalent in western culture, the relationship paradigm embraces the reality of paradox. Challenging and persistent problems are seen in their full complexity, and seen as deserving of the time needed to think through them in order to arrive at prudent responses. The result is a more thorough understanding of problems and a greater potential for finding answers that will work.

> Without some grasp of the meaning of their relationship to the whole, it is not easy for individuals to retain a vivid sense of their own capacity to act as individuals, a sureness of their own dignity, and an awareness of their roles and responsibilities. *— John Gardner*

This paradigm is changing the practice of leadership in the Episcopal Church. It is not a brand new concept; it was the guiding framework for developing the curricula for the Women of Vision (WOV) and GATES (Gaining Authority Through Education and Service). These two programs have been used with thousands of women all over the globe. Ann Smith, the former Executive Director of the Office of Women in Mission and Ministry, and I, along with several other colleagues, created the training materials and trained facilitators and presenters to use them. The programs reflect our shared vision of developing lay leaders capable of transformational and systemic change in the church and in the world, for we believe that change begins with individual formation and transformation and then ripples out to families, parishes, communities, the church, and ultimately the world. This pioneering effort in the early 1980s sowed the seeds for a different kind of participation and leadership from women in the Episcopal Church. The key lesson we all learned from this effort is that *transformation begins with the development of integrated leaders.* Many of the women who went through this training went on to serve on vestries, diocesan, provincial, and national leadership positions. These leaders began their journey of transformational change by engaging in the self-work Edwin Friedman has described as "self-differentiation." In the new Relationship Age paradigm it is called "inner work."

The future of the Episcopal Church rests with its ability to develop adaptive leadership capable of embracing paradox when complexity and ambiguity reign. It will need leadership that can hold these two major paradigms together and manage the tension that will inevitably result from doing so. Managing the tension of holding these two paradigms together requires a depth of self-knowledge that comes from engaging in an integrated approach to leadership development. Research in emotional intelligence shows that the capacity to engage in inner work is essential to achieving integrated leadership. Leaders with high emotional intelligence achieve their goals, affect the bottom line positively, and increase the performance of others. The familiar sarcasm and resistance that previously greeted inner work is ceasing, as research and experience demonstrate that this work creates both health and wealth in organizations.

Self-differentiated leaders who are in touch with themselves and conscious of the effect of their behavior on individuals and external environments are essential in the emerging Relationship Age paradigm. Society has been much more comfortable with the outer realm of leaders' lives because it is visible and measurable, and provides a sense of clarity as well as a measure of predictability and control. Numerous resources and tools exist to aid in assessing performance, production, and outcomes. What is needed are more resources and tools that help to develop and assess integrated, self-differentiated leaders. According to Dan Ciampa, advisor to business CEOs, 90 percent of the training leaders receive is technical while 90 percent of the challenges they face are adaptive. This disconnect is due in part to a stubborn cultural norm that has assigned demeaning and dismissive labels to the process of inner work. There are many programs that develop technical competencies but few that help form the critical adaptive capacities that are essential to the leadership work of transformation.

For some, engaging in self-awareness is perceived as a form of self-absorption, narcissism, and navel-gazing. But inner work is self-development for the sake of the world. It is more difficult because it deals with an invisible and frequently unconscious part of ourselves. I have observed only one clergyperson who consciously decided to destroy a community. The vast majority of clergy always intend to accomplish good, but the impact of a leader who is out of touch with herself will be unintentionally harmful. Self-awareness and knowledge can no longer be relegated to dismissive phrases like "touchy-feely" or "psychobabble," without realizing the consequences. Fortunately, in recent years more attention is being given to the development of the inner work of leadership.

> The process of becoming a leader is much the same as the process of becoming an integrated human being. For the leader, as for any integrated person, life itself is the career. — *Warren Bennis*

The integrated work of leadership reconnects and realigns the external world with the interior world. It integrates being with doing and utilizes both technical and adaptive skills to form a self-differentiated leader. The church needs leaders who are just as comfortable with and skilled at developing self-awareness as they are in completing a strategic plan. The church needs leaders who can hold the "tension of the opposites" together long enough to understand what the real problems are before deciding how to respond. To be able to do this work requires patience and centeredness, an inner core of stability, and the self-differentiation that is at the foundation of identity and vocation.

In our work with thousands of leaders in religion, business, philanthropy, and education, we have observed that they and their organizations are in varying stages of change and transition. They are in that time of no longer and not yet, that feared and dreaded in-between place that is like the desert experience. What is important for the future of the church is the cultivation of lay people and clergy who can lead others through these seismic shifts and changes, and who can exercise leadership in the new paradigm in ways that are cognizant and respectful of the past, knowledgeable of present reality, and courageous in envisioning a preferred future. This capacity is predicated on the authenticity and integrity of the leader, and this can be achieved only if the inner work is done and all the aspects of the leader's self are integrated. Accomplishing this means bringing together the content (*what* we teach) with the process (*how* we teach it).

Many of the existing leadership programs are content-heavy and/or process-light. Some drown people in words or let them become muddled in emotion. The first approach literally overwhelms people with data, in the belief that the more information that can be crammed into people, the better the program is perceived to be. It treats leaders like cars at a gas pump, waiting for their empty tanks to be filled. Since most people forget 80 percent of what they hear, in the long term the data-dump approach leaves participants initially satiated but ultimately dissatisfied. The assumption that those we teach are empty vessels leads to the creation of educational experiences that are mind-numbing and spiritually deadening. On the other hand, when the focus of education and development is primarily on process and light on content, the result is just as unsatisfying. This approach is much like focusing on waxing the car when the engine needs repair. Balancing substance with process is a sign that both inner and outer work are valued and that the goal is to develop truly integrated leaders capable of doing the challenging adaptive work.

At Christ Church in Raleigh, North Carolina, the adult Christian formation programs offered reflect the strong belief that members of the congregation are capable of pondering theological issues and are interested in attending programs that stimulate their intellectual *and* emotional needs. Their impressive offerings during the season of Lent are open to the greater community and are a spiritual feast for clergy and laity. Their former rector, Winston Charles, and the staff encourage continual learning and the use of knowledge to probe more deeply into the mysteries of faith and how we human beings choose to express our connection to the Divine.

External markers of success have been overemphasized in religious settings. While it is important for parishes to be outcomes-based and able to measure progress toward goals, technical measurements and outcomes-based approaches should not be made into demigods. How can the quality of relationships and pastoral care be measured by asking clergy to count the number of visits they make a week? Using objective measures as the sole indicators of how well a church is doing reduces the mission to a numbers game in which the core of the church's identity, authority, and vocation is seriously damaged.

At a morning service in one midwestern Episcopal parish, a long-time member went up to the altar to receive Holy Communion. She had just gotten up from kneeling and was still in prayer when the chair of the stewardship campaign stopped her to say she should get her pledge card in because the committee was nearing the deadline set for a particular goal. The parishioner was speechless. This same parish had posted a large United Way-like thermometer in the worship space near the baptismal font marking the degree to which it was moving toward the final goal, so perhaps it shouldn't have come as a surprise that she was tackled at the altar for the purposes of meeting a numerical goal.

At another parish, the chair of the stewardship campaign was the parish administrator. Before the vestry meeting, he approached a member because he had not yet turned in his pledge card. The vestry member had been an active member of the parish for thirty years and had always pledged. The administrator admonished him about the need to get his card in because they wanted to meet the goal of 100 percent participation on the vestry. When the man said he had always pledged and would be doing so again, the administrator retorted, "Your past history doesn't matter; it's the present that counts." The rector, who overheard this conversation, said nothing. Something was missing in the leadership of this parish and in its message about stewardship. Had there been theological preparation for those volunteering to conduct the stewardship campaign, this exchange would never have happened. The task of the parish administrator to obtain the pledge cards by a certain deadline was seen as a technical task, not an opportunity for spiritual exchange or relationship-building.

This is not to say that the technical skills needed in parish ministry are not important: organizing, planning, evaluating, communicating, running meetings, and fundraising—all of these technical skills contribute to the success of any initiative. But if they are not paired with adaptive skills, the result can be dehumanizing and offensive.

At St. Paul's Episcopal Church in Indianapolis, parishioners receive handwritten notes from members of the Stewardship Committee that share their own individual story of giving, and invite the recipient of the note to join them in giving. The volunteers are trained; their message is communal and theological, connecting people and reminding them of the reason for raising money. The notes are followed up with calls and/or visits.

Hundreds of Episcopal parishes participate in Stewardship Sunday. Those who treat the day as another marker in a financial goal rather than an opportunity to give thanks to God and to share in communion and community fail to teach the basic lesson of our faith—to love one another, as God loves us. Building up the body of Christ and accomplishing the mission of unity to which all of us are called means we must also be able to build relationships of trust that connect to the heart and spirit of God in ourselves and in our relationships with others. It means being able to hear our and their deepest desires and disappointments, helping all to find a sense of belonging, and then equipping them for ministry within and beyond their identified parish community. This inner and outer work is transforming leadership work, and the adaptive skills necessary to do it effectively are the subject of chapter 4. Before we turn to that work, however, we will look briefly at some of the ways that Episcopal churches on the margins can still provide fertile ground out of which such leadership will grow.

chapter three

On the Margin:
Promise and Possibility

*Blessed are those who trust in the LORD, whose trust is the
LORD. They shall be like a tree planted by water, sending
out its roots by the stream. It shall not fear when heat
comes, and its leaves shall stay green; in the year of
drought it is not anxious, and it does not cease to bear
fruit. (Jeremiah 17:7–8)*

We are a tradition centered in paradox. We know
from Scripture that in order to gain our lives we
must lose them, and the adaptive challenge in leadership
is to help people to remember this and realize that
through loss, new life comes. Most of the mainline
Protestant denominations are experiencing significant
losses—rising expenses, declining revenues, lower attendance, declining membership—so the Episcopal Church
is not alone. Whether these losses are ominous signs of
death is debatable; what is clear is that these denominations, once so central and influential in the lives of individuals and communities, are now "on the margin." In
matters of public debate and policy-making, the voice and

presence of the Episcopal Church is barely above a whisper. We can identify only a few religious leaders with any notable authority or influence in issues of public life, and with some there is a question of whether they are motivated by a care for the common good or their own egos and agendas.

Being on the margin can be seen as a place of loss and powerlessness, a void in which nothing happens and where no one can make a difference. But being on the margin can be more than a state of loss; it can be a place of transformation. Robert Lynn, retired Vice-President of Religion at the Lilly Endowment, hinted of this potential in his insightful observation that "the margin is not simply a displacement from former privilege." This conclusion is shared and described in "The Promise of the Margin," an essay written by Malcolm Warford, former President of Bangor Theological Seminary. The essay offers four descriptive frameworks from which to view the need for change in seminary education. The four frameworks—location, size, aim, and spirit—have been influential in my leadership work, and can be applied to understanding the current state of Episcopal Church and the implications for transformational change.

location

The significant societal and cultural shifts noted in the first two chapters have increased the awareness of the need for a different kind of leadership. They have forced multiple and diverse sectors to reexamine what is necessary to lead in this time of no longer and not yet. On the margin, leadership is defined more by character, integrity, and courage than by position, power, and status. This kind of leadership requires the ability to simultaneously be a part *of* a system while also being apart *from* it. So the experience of being on the margin can be an advantage in learning how to form transformational leaders and practice adaptive leadership skills. The margin allows leaders to see the parts and the whole and to grasp patterns and trends not easily seen from the center. Being on the margin may be the best *location* from which to develop the adaptive skills needed at this hinge of history. It exposes those in this place to a deeper understanding, a heightened awareness of complexity, a greater tolerance for chaos, and an enlightened capacity to discern and communicate meaning from voluminous facts. These characteristics probably sound familiar because they are the unique, though frequently forgotten or disputed, charisms that reside within the Episcopal Church. The ability to embrace paradox, the capacity to value diversity—of people, thoughts, and opinions—and to be truly inclusive are vestiges of our theological and spiritual heritage. The rich diversity found on the margin provides leaders with an opportunity to practice managing complexity and ambiguity, and to "hold the tension of the opposites." The margin is like the in-between time: it is the birthplace of possibilities, a crucible of change, and the place for practicing the universal dance between chaos and order. In it leaders learn to accept the reality of the present while simultaneously possessing a distinctive sense of a future not yet born.

Tensions are a part of community life; they should not distract us from asking, "What is the central work we are given to do?" —*Fredrica Harris Thompsett*

Being on the margin means having a changed perspective that comes from being dislocated from a position of centrality. Those in leadership on the margin can grasp the interconnectedness of people, events, and ideas, and see the unity that underlies all that God created, the unity to which we are all called. Well-integrated leaders possess a level of perception that provides those who follow with a much larger context in which to read and understand the church's historical evolution. It is a space of convergence between and among people who would not ordinarily have contact with each other. It is a point of contrasts where differences stand out in sharp relief, yet are an integral part of a larger pattern of relatedness. Literalism, theological insularity, and spiritual elitism are antithetical to the margin.

If being on the margin is owned as a place of preparation for leadership, transformation will have already begun. When claimed as a gift it shows the way to discern the Divine and omnipresent grace so easily ignored in the frenetic activity and confusion of change and reactionary-prone responses to chaos in the in-between state. Being on the margin is not a place of stasis or stability. It is one of prayerful discernment, deepening faith, fertile thoughts and ideas, and expectant waiting. This special location calls forth leaders who can be responsible critics, who can stand on the edge of two realities and figure out ways to bridge and transcend them. It is a place where wise answers to perplexing problems can be born and a vision and hope for a better world can be cultivated and disseminated. The promise of the margin is a gift the church can elect to receive.

size

Being on the margin can change the church's perspective on and strategies for growth. Many parishes experience a periodic tug of war between remaining their current size and getting bigger. The debate or dialogue juxtaposes cohesiveness and chaos, intimacy and isolation, vitality and stagnation, the status quo and death. The larger culture has valued everything BIG—big jobs, big bonuses, big institutions, supersized cars, supersized portions of food. Large size is equated with prosperity, with what is good.

The fixation on getting bigger has led to disastrous consequences, for several reasons. When the purpose for getting bigger is lost, getting bigger rather than better becomes the end goal. There are no boundaries, no framework for expectations that guide growth and provide it with meaning. Getting bigger in this instance is symptomatic of being muddled about mission. The ensuing lack of focus and absence of discipline leads to ineffectiveness. As Malcolm Warford reminds us, we "often get bigger because we aren't able to choose what really claims us." Conversations about church size and growth are important for congregations and clergy to have in order to ensure vitality and sustainability; but they must also help the leaders and members struggle with the question of "what really claims us," in order to decide how much and what kind of growth is needed.

God calls you to the place where the world's deep need and your deep gladness meet. —*Frederick Buechner*

It should be a given that what really claims the Episcopal Church is the mission to serve God. To stop at this level of explication is an abdication of responsibility and accountability. To unpack what claims us is to translate what it means to serve God in specific actions. Are these actions in alignment with our core faith beliefs? This line of questioning moves a congregation to examine what is precious, how it lives out its beliefs, and how it deploys its resources. It enables them to set boundaries that evolve from identity and are realistic. Some things will be done; some things will not. Some people will be helped; some will not. Establishing boundaries and setting priorities is an especially difficult task for church leaders, particularly in adverse economic conditions. The overwhelming majority of churches really care about meeting the needs of the poor, the hungry, and the homeless. However, the practice of responsible stewardship flows from clarity of identity and purpose and boundary-setting, not size.

> We must delight in each other, make others' conditions our own, rejoice together, mourn together, labor and suffer together, always having before our eyes our community as members of the same body.
> —*John Winthrop*

The church manifests God's love through its generosity to those in need. Providing food, clothing, and shelter to the poor is basic Christian charity. The intent is to alleviate suffering, but if the root causes of poverty are not also addressed, it is as if a glass of water is being poured on a blazing fire. The intent is to help, but the impact is miniscule. The practice of charity is insufficient to resolve the issues of hunger and poverty. An example of this can be seen in the practices of one well-known and highly respected parish that annually allocates $750,000 of its $30,000,000 endowment for outreach. The Grants Committee meets quarterly to decide on recipients of the parish grants, using previously agreed-upon criteria. The challenge is always whether to give a small amount to many organizations or larger amounts to a few. This dilemma is a painful one for the committee because although their grant fund is large, the needs presented for consideration always exceed the resources. Their practice is "to spread the money around as far as possible, and to give to program not administration." Focusing on size rather than impact is ineffective, and poor stewardship.

When it comes to Christian charity, size does matter. Small churches can have a huge impact if they focus, laser-like, on tackling major social problems. Conversely, large churches can have a minimal impact if their grant-making is spread so thin its effect is overshadowed by the need.

Outreach and grants committees often place such enormous constraints on grantee application processes it is hardly worth the time to apply. It is burdensome for many small, understaffed nonprofits to have to write multiple proposals and complete lengthy applications for a few dollars. The church should cease such practices. When intent matches impact, the size of a parish will not be the measure of its growth or greatness. It will make a difference because of the size of its vision and its laser-like focus and impact.

---

a i m

A third and related characteristic of being on the margin is *aim*—the setting of clear direction and establishing appropriate timelines for goals to be accomplished. A small rural parish in the Diocese of Indianapolis completed a beautiful new addition, along with some renovation to the sanctuary, all without going into debt. This was accomplished because the clergy leader saw the need and then listened to the congregation with patience. He took two years—the time needed to make sure the congregation was clear about why the renovation and expansion were necessary. He made sure that they understood the financial responsibility they would be shouldering. While the resulting physical facility is quite impressive, what is more notable is the congregation's sense of shared aim and fortitude in accomplishing it. When talking with their rector it was evident that his clear aim and steady presence was a major catalyst in this achievement.

Being on the margin is a place of many opportunities and options, and it is easy to be pulled in many directions. Having a clear aim can help followers get through difficult or challenging circumstances and to emerge with strength and joy. The lack of aim may well be one of the causes of the current state of "creative incoherence" cited by the Reverend William Sachs in his research on the Episcopal parishes and leadership. Parish leaders can identify the aim when they engage in honest self-evaluation, clarify their core values and beliefs, decide why and whom they exist to serve, and develop a compelling vision that captivates and aligns their theology with practice, their energy with intent, and their spirit with action. Aim gathers up the vast array of competing and conflicting interests and needs and helps to shape them into a coherent set of actions that can help the group accomplish its mission without becoming fragmented or scattered in its responses.

> Hospitality is not a subtle invitation to adopt the lifestyle of the host, but the gift of a chance for the guest to find his own. —*Henri Nouwen*

The ordering of priorities helps to align and direct energies. Being on the margin gives leaders the chance to determine the most effective ways to intervene in a system or to address a problem.

spirit

The fourth characteristic, *spirit,* is an invisible, intangible, yet vital aspect of leadership. It is an essential aspect of the health and well-being of any organization, especially the church. Spirit is an infusion of God's energy, the breath of life and joy in a community, the enthusiasm and courage that characterizes all its actions, and the context from which trust is developed. This understanding of spirit resides within the depths of individual psyches and in the foundations of organizational cultures. When we are tethered to this sense of spirit, the church will not succumb to quick-fix solutions and reactionary responses.

Regarding spirit, being on the margin means reaching for a fuller and deeper understanding of issues. It entails searching for meaning, demonstrating mendacity, exhibiting patience and independence, and being accountable. It is being rooted in humility so that when faced with the challenges of seemingly intractable issues, the church will have the courage to question what it "has always done" and let go of what has not worked in order to create a new future emboldened with a tenacious hope that it can and will make a difference.

Caring is the virtue that is born from the struggle to take responsibility. — *Eric Erikson*

Being on the margin is not a neat, orderly, antiseptic place. It is organic, messy, and unpredictable, but those who inhabit it learn that this is the birthplace where a new order can be born. It is fertile ground for redefinition and renewal. After the crucifixion of Jesus the fragile community of believers was thrown into the margin—the gap between what was and what is yet to come. Their location, size, and aim were not deterrents but enabled them to experience the in-between periods, to prepare to lead and to strengthen their faith and vision of transformation. On the margin: this is the place where the Episcopal Church currently resides, and it is the fertile place where the transformation of leadership can occur.

chapter four

The Call:
Leadership as Vocation

When a culture loses its authorized version, the body politic fragments, and its spiritual prosperity withers.
—*Bruno Bettelheim*

Although differences in polity and theology across the Anglican Communion seem irreconcilable at times, what I find constructive in this time of turmoil is that the current conflicts have precipitated a period of reexamination of identity and purpose. The church has been motivated, and in a few instances pushed, to identify what its beliefs are at the core and to create a common understanding from which to engage and reorder relationships with others in the Communion.

Soon after the 2003 General Convention of the Episcopal Church, the Episcopal Church Foundation interviewed over four hundred congregations. They discovered a lack of clarity about leadership, and that most did not have adequate resources or sufficient delivery systems to provide needed education and development. *The Search for Coherence,* the monograph based on the research by William Sachs, describes the church as being in a state of "creative incoherence." This is the result of old ways no longer working and a lack of the conviction and courage necessary to risk changing. The ensuing modern-day Tower of Babel reveals one of the challenges of being on the margin, of being in between the familiar and the yet-unborn, that of having vocational amnesia. The state of creative incoherence beckons us to return to our foundational sense of who we are and why we exist. It is a call to the vocation so movingly articulated in the Baptismal Covenant.

Will you continue in the apostles' teaching and fellowship, in the breaking of bread, and in the prayers?

The Baptismal Covenant conveys our Christian call; it is the contractual agreement addressing the universal questions of identity, our relationship to God, and our obligations to one another. In the reading of, listening to, and practicing of this sacred covenant we enter into the heart of God, a God who promises us community and connection, who holds and cradles us, a God who provides the peace and belonging we crave. We come to know an expectant God who asks us to fulfill our obligations to seek and serve Christ in all persons, to treat them with dignity and respect, and to persevere in resisting evil. When we are sent into the world "in peace, to love and serve the Lord," we are being sent out to live this covenant in some of the most challenging conditions. When asked whether we will seek to meet God's expectations in the covenant, we respond, "We will, with God's help." In this response we are expressing our strong desire to live out our baptismal promises, while knowing that we cannot enter into the gap between reality and the ideal without the help of the Divine.

The Baptismal Covenant calls us all to a common endeavor, and yet unless the deeper meaning of these words is translated into practical day-to-day actions, they lose their power to transform. The loss of meaning results in a state of creative incoherence—a state of hollow ritual and busyness lacking meaning. The church continues to clarify how the ministry of all the baptized should manifest itself. The working out of these shifting roles and relationships is vital in obtaining a creative, coherent state of leadership in the church.

Will you proclaim by word and example the Good News of God in Christ?

Implicit in the Baptismal Covenant is a template for the relationship and responsibilities of laity and clergy. It evokes shared leadership and mutual ministry that, when faithfully practiced, reinvigorates the church and expands its mission and impact across the globe. The Baptismal Covenant sees leadership in everyone and at every level. It claims a new paradigm of leadership, the DNA of which is embodied in the covenant.

Will you seek and serve Christ in all persons, loving your neighbor as yourself?

When the Israelites wailed in the desert, "What is to become of us?" they had forgotten who and whose they were and what they were called to do. The Israelites had lost the signposts that helped them to remember their identity and ultimate destiny, the guides that and provided them with security and direction. Likewise, the church is experiencing a passage of confusion and loss, and in our contemporary desert time the question of what is to become of us still hangs in the air. The Episcopal Church is in a period of crisis in leadership, a time of transition and preparation; if well used, this time will enable the church to see more clearly its aim and its vocation. The story of Exodus reminds us that in the in-between times, historical amnesia and loss of identity is a recipe for prolonged suffering.

We are being called to have the faith and courage to move through this time with grace-filled patience and trust, knowing that we will arrive at the Promised Land with God's help. Remembering our vocation, living out our Baptismal Covenant, will help us to endure and triumph.

Will you strive for justice and peace among all people, and respect the dignity of every human being?

The transformation of the church can be accomplished without losing what is precious to it, but it cannot avert change. Whether it is accepting a revised *Book of Common Prayer* or the service leaflet in its place, the loss of an esteemed lay or clergy leader or the departure of parishes and splitting of dioceses, a period of grief and disorientation will ensue. Any time our understanding of identity, authority, and vocation is called into question, the real work is to live into and through the dissonance that automatically comes with change, emerging with an even stronger faith.

This is work that cannot be done alone; learning to do the work of transformation requires a community of faithful learners and leaders. The church should be the primary institution preparing leaders for this work. If it accepts this vocation the church will enter a "renaissance of mission" that will revitalize the church and plant the seeds of transformation in the world.

We will need a set of skills and resources designed to bring about such transformation. The resources described on the following pages will enable leaders to read differing historical and cultural realities deftly, to develop competence in group dynamics and development, and to gain expertise in facilitating adaptive work. Additional skills in managing change and resolving conflict, translating facts into a meaningful narrative, creating communities of learning, engendering cultures of trust, and manifesting courage, integrity, and authenticity will be essential.

---

understanding organizational culture

In addition to the larger societal, global, and historical contexts described in chapter 1, obtaining a broader and deeper understanding and knowledge of organizational culture is critical to the work of transformation. Culture is a complex concept, and its creation and ongoing development is one of the key responsibilities of the new leadership. The ability to read culture and to manage the complexity of human and organizational experiences and perspectives that exist within it is the *sine qua non* of leadership.

In *Organizational Leadership and Culture,* Edgar Schein defines culture as a pattern of shared basic assumptions learned by a group as it solved problems of external adaptation and internal integration. These shared basic assumptions are those that have proven to be successful and valid, and that infuse those new to the culture with the appropriate way to perceive, think, and feel in addressing future problems.[1]

Terry Deal, coauthor of *Corporate Cultures* and an expert observer of systems, describes culture as, "The way we do things around here." This pithy aphorism captures the behavioral aspects of culture, while Schein's more intricate definition points to the deeper underlying structures and unconscious assumptions that frequently evolve into unquestioned beliefs and unexamined behaviors. Both of these definitions of culture compose a hologram through which we can view how a parish perceives, believes, and thinks about itself, how it is perceived by the larger public, and the impact of these perceptions on mission. The following typology might assist in exploring the depth and breadth of culture that the most effective leaders learn to master. The levels indicate the degree of visibility.

A TOOL FOR READING ORGANIZATIONAL CULTURE

	LEVELS	FOCUS	LEADERSHIP ROLE
EXTERNAL	ARTIFACTUAL	Literature, image, attire, rituals, public materials	Public face of the organization's mission and message; myth maker
	STRUCTURAL	Organization, structure, distribution of resources, space utilization, markets, production	Enabler of competence, manager, administrator
INTERNAL	BEHAVIORAL	Management of people, trust, relationships, communication	Creator of community, skill-builder, educator
	PHILOSOPHICAL	Management of values, beliefs, vocation, mission, philanthropic interests, community	Creator of culture, storyteller, connector of ideas and actions, interpreter, translator
	FOUNDATIONAL	Basic assumptions about existence, purpose, relationship to larger world, spirituality	Meaning-maker, creator of spiritual model for authenticity and integrity, integration, groundedness

THE ARTIFACTUAL LEVEL OF CULTURE

The artifactual level showcases the obvious and visible aspects of culture most easily associated with an organization. For a church these include the physical location, architecture, worship space, placement of the altar, furnishings, and art, as well as tangible aspects of church life such as the service bulletins, website, nametags, bulletin boards, and newsletters. We can gain some understanding of a parish culture through observing such phenomena.

At this level of culture, status and authority are equated with formal position, title, and institutional name. The leader can easily become the personification of the parish and the bearer of its institutional myth. The identity of the leader and that of the parish can merge into a blended image of projections from past experiences and unspoken expectations of parish members. Differentiating between projection and reality is important in the work of transformational leadership. Differentiation means that the leader will be able to clearly know the difference between who they are and whom others believe them to be. One of the hallmarks of transformational leadership is the ability to differentiate self from institutional *persona* while still accepting the role of institutional narrator, a responsibility that paradoxically requires more than the ability to tell the institution's story; it involves knowing and telling the leader's own story. The *deeper* knowledge of self prevents the seduction of a leader to believe automatically either the accolades or criticisms.

One tool we use to help tell the individual and the institutional story is TimeScape,© a history timeline and set of exercises that provide a powerful process for obtaining the parish's history and its developmental trajectory. These exercises help a congregation and its leaders to separate myth from fact, identify core values and beliefs, surface organizational strengths and weaknesses, and build and strengthen community.

The creation of the TimeScape© should involve all of the parishioners. We suggest establishing a committee of five to six representatives from the parish to serve as a Resource Committee. This group will be responsible for researching the parish's documented and observed history. It will also organize and conduct interviews with the members of the parish and a cross-section of designated diocesan and community members and leaders. The data gathered will be shared with the whole parish or in a retreat setting with the vestry. All groups have the opportunity to add more information to the timeline.

A Tool for Understanding History: TimeScape©
St. Francis-in-the Fields, a suburban Episcopal parish, was entering a significant transition triggered by the ending of a five-year strategic plan and the impending retirement of their beloved rector. The senior warden and the rector called to ask for help in planning and preparing for the future. The fact that they made the call together was a very healthy sign. The parish vestry was struggling with whether the congregation should be looking toward the future at the same time they might be embarking on a search for a new clergy leader. The date of the current rector's retirement was not set and no one dared to bring up the subject in the group for fear of offending the well-liked and accomplished leader.

They learned in a review of parish history that their rector was unable to be more specific about a date because she was still in the process of deciding what she wanted to do and how she wanted to leave. In working with this group, preparing a TimeScape© of the parish helped them see how much had been accomplished, how much they had grown, and the achievements and challenges with which they were now entrusted. A photo gallery of significant parish events was displayed on tables around the room.

As the retreat began, vestry and staff members signed their names on the timeline at the point when they first became aware of the parish, when they became involved, and when they became a member. As they signed in they added additional events, issues, and people to the timeline. After each person signed in, the group listened to the "founding story" of the parish. The founding story carries the origins of the parish vision and mission, reveals the core values and beliefs that are the DNA of parish ministry, and conveys the character of its leadership and the nature of its culture. The group members were then called upon in the order in which they signed in. Every person shared when they first came to the parish and why, what they knew about the parish at the time, what the significant issues and events were, and who were the key people. During this process the individual stories were woven into the parish story.

> We must always remember that our sense of what is real or true is a complex process that involves intentional reflection, the discipline of deep discernment, responsible questioning, inquiry of individual and collective experiences and practices. It includes an examination of our ideas, assumptions, beliefs, attitudes, and behaviors. The truth of what we see, what we come to know, and who we are coming to be are always shaped by a complex interaction between the internal and the external realms of our lives. —Katherine Tyler Scott

This exercise brought together three sources of parish history: what people remembered, what was documented, and what was observed. The shared historical narrative left members feeling much more connected, cohesive, and energized. The reflections on the history created a shared knowledge of the parish culture and the people and forces that shaped it. It also provided insight into the deeper levels of culture where unquestioned assumptions are stored and behavioral patterns in congregational life are rooted. Listening to the reasons why members came to the congregation touched the nerve center of the congregation—the craving for purpose and meaning and a yearning for a life lived in faith and mission.

A parish's history reveals the human and universal search for meaning and belonging, and identifies who and what is most important in the unfolding formation of individuals and organizations. It is also a process that simultaneously affirms the strengths of parish life and culture, while identifying the issues that need further attention and work. This particular parish's vestry and staff were able to celebrate the many successes and could affirm and appreciate their leader in a way that allowed them to begin to let go and plan for a future without one another.

This parish is continuing to mature and grow as it prepares for this major leadership transition with increased confidence and a renewed commitment to their mission. Their timeline has been computerized and made available to engage new members as they continue the important conversation about the ongoing development of identity, mission, and community. Because they worked on their history they are better prepared to call their next leader.

THE STRUCTURAL AND BEHAVIORAL
LEVELS OF CULTURE

Both the structural and behavioral levels of culture unearth tangible forms of the organization of people and worship, and how congregants participate in ministry inside the parish and out in the world. The weekly and annual calendars of parish activities, the worship bulletins, and an organizational chart are all indicators of how the leadership and life of a parish are ordered. If these artifacts do not exist, this is also important information about parish culture.

Vestry and committee meetings are other venues that help a leader to decipher communication dynamics and patterns, mission, and the distribution and exercise of power. Questions that can be asked of such gatherings include:

- How are members orientated? prepared to lead?
- Who convenes the meeting?
- Who attends?
- Who plans the agenda?
- How often and where do they meet?
- When and how do the meetings begin?
- How is leadership experienced?
- What opportunities are there for Bible study and/or theological reflection?
- What frameworks and norms exist for discussion and decision-making?
- How is mission integrated?

The answers to questions such as these are very revealing about the culture of a parish.

Another way to access these two levels of culture is to attend the ubiquitous coffee hour following a parish worship service, and consider the following questions:

- How do people hear about it?
- Where is it located? How accessible is it?
- What time is it scheduled?
- Who attends?
- What are people given to eat and drink?
- Do the clergy attend? With whom do they talk?
- Are nametags available, and are they worn?
- How are visitors greeted, and then treated?
- How are members treated?

When my husband and I first moved to the Diocese of Indianapolis, we visited every parish in the deanery searching for a home. One Sunday we visited a parish that to our surprise had the bishop visiting them. When we walked into the church, no one looked at or greeted us. We found our seats and sat in observant silence. We were barely greeted during the Peace and, after a beautiful service, we processed out to attend the reception. Members joyfully greeted one another and gathered in clusters of familiar friends. The bishop spotted us and came over to hug us. His huge smile and embrace of us was food for our souls and a gesture of our friendship. No one in this congregation knew he was a friend of ours until that moment. After this, a number of people came up to say hello and to welcome us. As we left to go home, we looked at each other and knew that we would not return to this parish. The structural elements of the culture were exactly what we expected—everything was identifiably Episcopalian—but the behavior of the congregants was the antithesis of an inclusive, hospitable, loving community. We immediately learned that in this parish status mattered more than the Baptismal Covenant.

You yourselves are our letter, written on our hearts, to be known and read by all; and you show that you are a letter of Christ, prepared by us, written not with ink but with the Spirit of the living God, not on tablets of stone but on tablets of human hearts. *(2 Corinthians 3:2–3)*

These levels of culture require leadership with excellent organizational and planning skills. They need leaders with strong administrative skills and the ability to match people and resources in ways that maximize the parish's ability to accomplish its mission. Even when there is staff designated to do this work, the rector must be capable of supervising the work. The clergy leader is responsible for the workings of the whole system and its parts, and serves as the "creator of community." Creating an environment in which people feel purpose, belonging, a shared identity, security, and trust is a responsibility that sets the transforming leader apart from others.

An example of this kind of leadership can be seen in a healthy and growing parish that is part of a diocese experiencing budgetary problems and chronic leadership lethargy. The rector recognized the need to attract younger individuals and families and began by first educating the vestry about the need to do this. Although this highly successful congregation seemed an unlikely candidate for major change, this rector was able to show the congregation its future through a study of demographics in the Episcopal Church. He engaged the vestry in analyzing the research data and its implications for the parish. Once the vestry members understood the urgency, and realized that the initiative was not about "fixing a failure" but about ensuring the future, they supported the change and the hiring of a staff person to develop programs and services for this demographic.

The message was clear: "We are serious about our ministry to young individuals and families." The parish is seeing a revitalization of youth programs, and more activities for young parents and children are planned. This particular leader framed this initiative in ways that helped all of the parish feel included in this process of forming a culture of lifelong learning so that everyone, from cradle to maturity, could see that their formation is always important, even as more resources and attention were being provided to a younger demographic.

THE PHILOSOPHICAL LEVEL OF CULTURE

The fourth level of culture is not so easily or directly ascertained as that of the structural and behavioral levels. This is the place of unquestioned assumptions and unchallenged core beliefs and values. Most of the behaviors at the philosophical level are unconscious, yet they have an enormous effect on the community of a parish. This level is deeper than what we can see, and it goes to the heart of *why* a congregation gathers to worship. It is where the meaning of the more visible and outward signs of life in a faith community exists.

An example of this level is the way in which a congregation "passes the Peace." This act reveals deeply held values and beliefs about the ecclesial responsibility for creating relationships and a community of belonging. It is a manifestation of a congregation's beliefs about physical touch and connection, the role of worship, the importance of community, and the meaning of the Eucharist. During the passing of the Peace in one parish, nearly all of the people move fluidly across and up and down the aisles, erupting into quiet but brief exchanges, hugging, smiling, and greeting warmly all whom they encounter. In another parish the parishioners pass the Peace only to those who are in their immediate proximity. In still another congregation a number of people remain kneeling in prayer during the passing of the Peace. These practices reflect the cultural differences that lie at the deeper levels of parish life.

An examination of why a parish engages in certain practices is a way to ensure that there will not be a disconnect between the activities of a parish and the beliefs they espouse as precious or unchanging. Without congruence between their values and actions, parishes can lose a sense of integrity, and can easily become overextended and frenzied in their program offerings. Actions and activities that are not tethered to core values can easily lead to forms of institutional narcissism, meaningless group activity, and mission silos. They may possess the trappings of community but lack the substance and meaning of what makes a community.

THE FOUNDATIONAL LEVEL OF CULTURE

The last level of culture is what I call the foundational level, and is very close to the philosophical level, but it is far less visible. Core values and faith identity reside here; this is the level of spiritual depth in which something greater and more powerful than anyone or anything is encountered. This level houses the basic assumptions about why we exist, our purpose and reason for being, and our relationship to the Divine. It is the place of connection to a larger reality and a transcendent circle of belonging, a place of deep knowing in which we understand and feel that we are all part of the same Divine Source of all life.

This deeply spiritual and transcendent place has no easy or direct route to it. It can't be commanded or demanded to appear but is most accessible through attention to the other levels of culture and through a disciplined practice of reflection, prayer, meditation, and the study of Scripture. The special responsibility and vocation of clergy is to access this level on a regular basis and to model for followers the practices and discipline that will take them to deeper places of understanding and connection to God.

Many of us have experienced the gift of grace and congruence in which we feel connected to the Divine. I recall a beautiful homily at the ordination of a priest that left the congregation breathless and in awe, or the experience of my parish when our building was undergoing renovation and we were invited to worship on a glorious Easter Sunday in a Jewish synagogue. The ability to cross such divides and be in relationship and unity with those whom we may usually see as only different was a taste of the transcendent, of what heaven is. These experiences not only leave us speechless, but inspired and full of hope that we might be able to live out God's love after all.

We have also likely experienced times when actions are not synchronous with what is said or believed:

* a parish perceives itself as warm and friendly but does not greet newcomers at coffee hour;

* church members express discomfort when a homeless, disheveled person wanders into the Sunday service;

* volunteers are not given adequate meeting space or the resources necessary to carry out an assignment;

* lay leaders are engaged in diocesan and national mission but are offered no parish support;

* members serve in positions of responsibility indefinitely without being given an honorable out;

* lay employees are offered pay and benefits that are close to or below the poverty level.

If disconnects such as these are not recognized and resolved over time, the incongruence between actions and the foundational beliefs and values deepens and widens, leaving a groove of undifferentiated and chronic dis-ease, a pernicious form of cynicism, and a significant erosion of trust in the authenticity of the clergy and the congregation.

In one urban parish with which we worked, there was a large network of guilds and *ad hoc* program groups, each with its own distinctive history, agenda, and fundraising activities. Each group felt it was contributing to the mission of the parish and serving legitimate needs. There was poor communication and little or no collaboration between them. The larger purpose of the church and its mission of unity in Christ had become buried in a thicket of competitive activities and endless meetings.

Understandably, the newly-called rector wanted to disband these traditional and often competitive groups.

He felt they were "a drag on the mission" even though there appeared to be a strong allegiance to them in the parish. Our counsel was to start with first understanding the history and the existence of guilds as a way to obtain valuable data about the culture. The rector and the vestry could then better determine what should be retained and what should not.

> It is time we attend to the formation of the character of leaders and the cultures which they help to create and which, in turn, help to create them. We must cultivate and strengthen the connections between the being and doing of leaders so that our leadership improves the character of individuals and the culture of organizations and the communities they serve.
> — *Katherine Tyler Scott*

The rector visited the guilds and groups, observed their activities, talked with the members, and learned a lot about them and the parish itself. Because he took the time to understand the history and more accurately read the culture, he was able to understand how the guilds and groups had come into being, how they had veered away from the larger purpose, and how they had become disconnected from the deeper roots of the parish's mission.

The adaptive work of this rector was to realign the beliefs and actions. He invited the groups' leaders to weekly Bible study and created opportunities to bring them together on projects that served the whole parish. He also started a new group for professional working women that met in the evenings rather than during the day. This opened up the membership, and the groups began to become less resistant to change. In doing so, they began to collaborate, and eliminated the duplication of projects and constant fundraising efforts.

Another example of the capacity to operate from a foundational level of culture that enabled the leader to read the larger reality and to see issues in a deeper and broader context is a meeting of diocesan leaders after the General Convention of 2003. Each one expressed a feeling of being weary from the fractious dialogue over same-sex blessings. The group was preparing for an upcoming diocesan convention. Several members voiced their opinions about some of the General Convention legislation passed in response to the Windsor Report.

After sharing their thoughts about the upheaval and threats of schism in some quarters of the Episcopal Church and in the Anglican Communion, one individual characterized the problem as "the African bishops intervening in our business when they have no moral authority themselves." Another stated cavalierly that "it's just a few parishes that will end up leaving." Additional comments revealed that few had read the full report or had a complete understanding of the General Convention's legislative process. Fewer still had much of an understanding of the history of the Anglican Communion or knew what was meant by the "Instruments of Unity." Many saw the unfolding events in non-negotiable terms of right and wrong or good and bad.

The ordained leaders present at the meeting made no comment and did not attempt to correct the ignorance and misinformation. The result was that an opportunity for learning passed. No offer was made to provide a theological rationale to explain why the General Convention voted the way it did or why we now face tensions in the Anglican Communion regarding unity and identity.

As I watched this exchange I wondered if anyone would leave this meeting with a sense of wanting to read and learn more about the issues to challenge their ignorance. I was uncomfortably surprised at how little the clergy had done to educate congregants or to expand their understanding of a larger context. In another congregation the rector extracted one paragraph from the one-hundred-plus-page Windsor Report to explain what it meant to the vestry members and used this slice of data to justify the position he had already taken. At another parish meeting, in which the clergy had been asked to discuss the recommendations in the report in a more in-depth manner, a vestry member said in an exasperated and defiant tone, "Who the h____ are these people?" This profane expression of a question was an opportunity to learn about the Anglican Communion, the polity of the Episcopal Church, its identity and culture, and to engage the vestry and the congregation in the adaptive work of examining their biases. It was a teaching moment, but the clergy responded with silence, followed with a pronouncement that these people have no real authority over the American church.

As the conversation continued, a number of the members took the lead of the clergy and said that it mattered little to them "what others in the Anglican Communion think about what the U.S. church does." They insisted that they "will continue doing what they have always done." These responses ignored the swirling winds of theological debate threatening to blow the Anglican Communion off its foundations. To avoid engagement in real work (and to further their own agenda) the leaders exploited the ignorance of the group. When clergy and lay leaders engender and cultivate rigid, myopic views of major issues, they place their congregations and organizations in danger of becoming closed enclaves of self-obsession and righteousness having no strong connection to the larger family of faith. We can disagree and still belong in the community when tinderbox issues arise if we have leaders who are theologically, intellectually, and spiritually prepared to help others gain understanding.

Fredrica Harris Thompsett's observation in *We Are Theologians* bears repeating here: "With so much going on in our society and world, *what* we choose to notice reveals *who* we are." Traditionally, Episcopalians are called to understand a wider reality and be able to fully engage in a panoply of differing opinions and positions. This practiced discipline means that our leaders must have the capacity to hold the "tension of the opposites" together. They are to help the congregation pay attention to what is relevant and essential, and to remember that what is paid attention to affects identity and calling. Can the church minister to the world with authenticity and integrity when it denies these tensions and refuses to contribute to understanding?

The church is being called to pay attention to the current state of "creative incoherence" that William Sachs discovered in his research. The mind-numbing busyness in some parishes and the beautiful trappings and symbols that are treasured in others will not in the long run be a substitute for the search for answers to the ancient, universal, and profound vocational and mission questions we all experience: Who are we? For what purpose do we exist? What are we called to do? They are profoundly and deeply religious in nature. Those in positions of leadership in the church are charged with the primary responsibility to create opportunity and spaces in which to wrestle with these questions.

A Tool for Understanding Philanthropy

Every parish includes some form of outreach in its definition of identity and mission, but these efforts can become imprisoned in unquestioned assumptions and unexamined mission activities. For example, giving multiple small grants to community organizations on the front lines of serving the most needy—organizations teetering on the edge of survival themselves—can be torturous and burdensome. If a parish requires completion of a ten-page application form with stringent guidelines for evaluation and annual reporting on tiny grants, a discussion is in order. What is the understanding of outreach? Stewardship? Accountability? What impact can be realistically expected from a $1,000 grant to an organization that has the responsibility to address serious and intractable problems such as poverty, inadequate education, homelessness, and a lack of health care?

Understanding the different traditions of philanthropy and making a conscious decision about which one the parish must practice is a first step in making what is implicit explicit. A schema developed by D. Susan Wisely, former Director of Evaluation at The Lilly Endowment, defines three major philanthropic traditions: charity, improvement, and social reform.

PHILANTHROPIC TRADITIONS

	CHARITY	IMPROVEMENT	SOCIAL REFORM
PRINCIPLE	Compassion	Progress	Justice
GOAL	Alleviates human suffering	Maximizes human potential	Encourages social change
STRATEGY	Benevolence	Education	Problem-solving
ADDRESSES	Basic and immediate needs	Individual and group capacity	Systemic change

Used by permission of D. Susan Wisely

Transforming leaders examine the foundational level of parish culture to determine which tradition is embedded and influences practices in the parish. For example, if charity is the tradition of giving in a parish, the primary intent is to alleviate suffering. The compassion for someone in immediate need recognizes the state of crisis and guides the desire to give *now*. If the tradition is improvement of the lives of those in need, then the strategy changes to one of equipping the individual or group with the capacity to improve their lives through education and opportunities. The initiative can begin in the now, but it will take time for change to happen. The third tradition of giving is social reform, the intent to change the system that creates and perpetuates the problem. In this instance, the primary strategy is a long-term effort requiring focused investment of time, money, and people resources.

Each of these strategies has an impact, but not all of them will be transformative in nature. Each one progressively requires more of the involvement of the donor; each one requires increasing levels of adaptive skills, those skills required when the problem is complex and unclear and the leader must engage those with the problem in resolving it. The questions with which parish leaders will need to wrestle include:

- What are our guiding principles?
- What are the implicit assumptions in our actions?
- What is our mission and vocation?
- What is the ultimate impact that we want our giving to have?
- Who is it that we are intending to serve?
- Are our actions congruent with our values?

These classifications of philanthropic practice provide a framework within which parishes can address these questions, evaluate their philosophy and mission of giving, and determine the desired impact. This is a responsible way the church can determine if it is engaged in transformational work and whether it has the right leadership in place to accomplish it.

The Reverend Kent Millard, minister at St. Luke's Methodist Church, Indianapolis, shares his parish culture's view of philanthropy and practice in these words: "Money is *never* an excuse for not doing something; if it is of God, the money will be there." Money is not the plumb line for successful outreach; a passion for God and service to others is. The staff and congregation believe in the abundance of God. Congregants and potential grantees are not required to complete lengthy forms or appear before committees in order to receive approval and support. Accountability exists and it is grounded in a theology of prosperity and abundance. The values fit the actions.

Leadership is the fundamental process by which culture is formed and transformed, and the leader is the chief architect of culture. This means also having an understanding of the dynamics of change and how to manage it. Transformational leadership requires an understanding of how individuals, organizations, and communities respond to change.

---

leading change

The gap between ending the current reality and moving others into the preferred reality is the most challenging task for a leader who desires transformation. We know that the leader of transformational change must know the institutional story, the organization's historical trajectory over time, and the mega-narrative in which the organization's capacity for managing change resides. This capacity emerges from the key changes the organization has experienced, how it responded to these changes, and what organizational learning occurred as a result. Determining the parish's ability to manage change reveals the strengths upon which to build as well as the weaknesses.

The most effective leaders of change are not only historians; they are analysts and prophets too. Once they understand the past and have read the larger reality in which they live, they can use their assessment to find the best way to proceed to the preferred future. This plan needs to be inspired by vision and translated into a blueprint for change that clearly explicates the urgency for change, the purpose and goals, and the strategies for achieving success. A thorough assessment and analysis can also reveal the degree of change being proposed and how to anticipate and deal with the ways the changes will affect particular individuals or groups of people.

Most advocates of change initiatives focus on the changes they are trying to produce and fail to recognize the importance of learning capabilities. —*Peter Senge*

The leader of transformational change is aware of both the type of change induced and level of culture that will be most affected. This awareness will help determine the most effective strategies for launching and managing successful change. The leader's assessment of the organization's capacity, readiness, and skill level is essential. It may be prudent to begin with lower risk, technical, or structural interventions as preparation for more transformative change if the congregation has had little experience with managing change successfully.

The deeper levels of organizational culture demand a higher level of skills. Clergy are not omnipotent, and expecting them to do and be everything is a setup for failure. Acknowledging their limitations and their gifts can liberate them to learn to appreciate and use the gifts and skills already present in the parish community. Acknowledging both gifts and limitations reduces a leader's blind spot and provides a broader, more comprehensive picture of what the leadership in the parish needs in order to bring about transformational change.

Change is a constant reality and managing and leading it is a huge challenge for leaders. Change at any level of culture stresses an organization. The degree of stress is dependent on the degree of change, and if change stirs up questions about identity and mission, then the leader has to understand the psychological effects precipitated by change.

ORGANIZATIONAL RESPONSES TO CHANGE

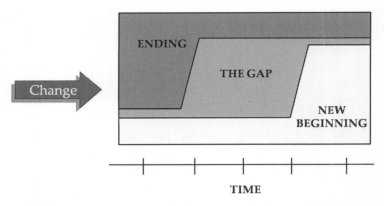

Organizations generally experience three phases of change:

Phase One: The Ending
Phase Two: The Gap
Phase Three: The New Beginning

Whenever major change in a congregation is introduced, this transition process begins, unleashing many psychological states within individuals in the parish. For leaders who are managing and leading change, it is imperative to understand what these are.

Phase One: The Ending
The introduction of change is felt as an ending by the majority of people. Nearly 75 percent of them will be in a state of denial and resistance. About 10 percent will have already moved into Phase Two, and the remainder will be in Phase Three. The leader of change is what I call a Phase Three Leader, trying to influence those who are opposed to change. If such leaders do not understand this gap, their actions may end up reinforcing the Phase One emotions.

Phase Two: The Gap
In this phase change is experienced as a time of ambiguity, anxiety, and confusion. A variety of emotions are experienced in this phase, from hating the change to already living it. In any given parish experiencing major transition, over time more people will move into this phase, as fewer people remain in the earlier phase of denial and resistance.

Phase Three: The New Beginning
In Phase Three about 75 percent of the congregants have embraced the new beginning, while about 10 percent remain in the Gap and 10 percent remain in denial and resistance. If everything has been done to bring people along toward the new vision, the challenge for a leader in this phase is to focus on those who have embraced the change. This is the big "if," because coercing or cheerleading change will not work in the first two phases. People are in shock and grief, and their emotions and the level of anxiety make it difficult to be persuaded by reasoned logic.

The leader's task in bringing about transformation is to help people let go. Leadership and change consultant William Bridges says that most change initiatives fail because the work of letting go is ignored. Rushing people through the phases only contributes to regression and a weakened commitment to the desired change.

MANAGING THE CHANGE PROCESS

An inability to assess and analyze the culture completely and accurately can lead to an intervention that communicates an unintended message to an organization. This happened in one parish when the priest-in-charge hired a strategic planner with considerable background in corporate planning but with no knowledge of or experience with the Episcopal Church. The intended message of the importance of a disciplined approach to planning for mission became blurred and bogged down in a confusing parade of exercises and incomprehensible reports devoid of the spirit and grace needed to revitalize this congregation.

Matching an intervention to a particular level of culture and phase of change is important. If this is not done, it can look as though the leader is impervious to the true needs of followers and lay leaders. In one corporate-sized parish the members of the altar guild always met briefly with the priest for prayer just before the service, and after the service the priest would hand his vestments to them and warmly thank them for their service. This ritual, developed over the years, was more than a pastoral expression of gratitude; to the guild members it was an affirmation of their ministry, and it had come to have significant meaning. When a new priest arrived, he decided it was more efficient to vest and disrobe in his office. He did not talk with the guild members, so he was unaware of their practice and its meaning. When several members of the guild gathered enough courage to talk with the priest about this change, he perceived their efforts as an attempt to control him. He held his ground and in the process destroyed something precious in that community and in the relationship between the priest and

the lay leaders: the recognition and affirmation of vocation. The priest's ignorance of the parish tradition, along
with the historical mythology of powerful altar guilds he
brought with him, made it impossible for him to see the
spiritual significance of this practice. This leader missed
an opportunity to learn the deeper level of meaning in this
church's subculture. On the surface, the change seemed
inconsequential, but this misunderstanding of the intent
and impact of a particular tradition created a rift between
the priest and those in the altar guild.

Whatever the level at which change is introduced, the
leader's task is to ensure that as much alignment and
congruence as possible exists between the types of change
and the levels of culture. This engenders trust in leadership, and enables those who are being asked to change to
leave their comfort zones and take the necessary risks to
achieve personal and organizational transformation.

The ability to deal with change requires special
training. Reading this chapter is a good beginning, but
intentional education and coaching in developing these
skills is essential. A list of organizations that provide work-
shops and educational programs, as well as excellent
consultants who can assist leaders and parishes in dealing
with change, is included in the resource section of this
book. Intentional professional development and adaptive
leadership skills training is transformational, and the
leaders who undertake the vocation to lead change
provide an enduring contribution to the church.

chapter five

The Sacramental Nature of Leadership

So we, though many, are one body in Christ, and individually members one of another. Having gifts that differ according to the grace given to us, let us use them.
(Romans 12:5–6, RSV)

The clarion call for church leadership is occurring at a time of enormous societal change. In addition to the three major changes noted in chapter 1, we are witnessing any number of shifting realities:

◆ an ever-widening gap between the poor and the wealthy;
◆ a persistent, low-grade hostility toward difference;
◆ a slow, steady decline of relationship networks that form the foundation for community cohesion and problem-solving;
◆ a loss of shared identity and belonging;
◆ a rise in individualism and insularity;
◆ a decrease in the public's trust in leaders and institutions;

◆ a continuing retreat into privatization of public services;
◆ economic volatility, the rising costs of healthcare, pervasive poverty, and increased competition for resources.

In addition to these changes, the historic divides of race, class, and gender continue in varying degrees, making the litany of problems and grim statistics sobering.

The previous chapters cited several examples of congregational leaders who have not retreated from this litany of significant changes and challenges. What is it that contributed to their belief that they could make a meaningful difference in situations frequently filled with anxiety and stress? Why do they continue to support struggling outreach programs? What gives them the sense that they can overcome intolerance and prejudice and open up communities walled off by privilege and ignorance? What is it that makes them continue to reach out to change abject conditions and refuse to surrender to adversity? More than any one thing, I believe it is the capacity to see their leadership as spiritually based—indeed, as *sacramental.*

It is difficult to live the words of Paul to the church in Rome quoted above, and the church finds it even more difficult to manifest the belief that we are indeed "one body in Christ, and individually members one of another" in times of complex change and uncertainty. We must remember, however, that the history and shape of community has always been influenced by religious values and beliefs. It is through religious institutions and leaders that Americans give expression to the belief that we have a shared responsibility for one another. Much of our voluntary service is motivated by religious belief and civic responsibility. Inherent in community service and philanthropy is the expectation that citizens in a democracy have a responsibility to be involved in identifying and addressing the concerns and issues of their communities and of the world.

The value Americans have placed on voluntary action for the public good was, and is, integral to an understanding of who we are as citizens and as Christians. In living out the historical legacy of caring for those less fortunate we experience the pull and tug between self-interest *and* the common good. Alexis de Tocqueville, in *Democracy in America,* described our penchant for individualism as "a calm and considered feeling which disposes each citizen to isolate themselves from the masses and withdraw into a circle of family and friends; with this little society formed to their tastes, they gladly leave the greater society to look after itself." He also said that the danger of individualism was that it could lead to "being shut up in the solitude of our own hearts." The tension we experience is in the desire for autonomy and the reality of our interdependence. Leadership that is transformational recognizes this paradox-induced tension and strives to temper unfettered individualism and the tyranny of the majority. Transformational leadership accepts responsibility for holding these tensions and enables followers to manage the ambiguity and anxiety long enough to obtain a balanced perspective that avoids self-sacrifice or pious isolation.

Perhaps the most challenging work for church leaders in our time is confronting the hard lines drawn between our private and public lives that deplete both sectors of the full use of ourselves in service to mission. Dichotomies and divides between people persist and can threaten the emergence and sustainability of the kind of community Paul imagined. We are in danger of losing the meaning of an inclusive community; in too many instances we have retained the "habits" of community but have lost the "heart" of it. The loss of community parallels the demise of language that expresses our interdependence and our vision of unity. How can the church cultivate a deeper understanding of shared responsibility to hold others in trust—to care for those we may never know, in a time we will never see? How can we help reclaim the necessary habits and practices that flow from understanding that we are all "one body in Christ"?

In the work we have done with civic, philanthropic, business, and religious leaders, I have seen many whose deepest desire is to strengthen the core values, character, and commitment to service of their staff, members, and other constituents. Their desire is to improve the quality of life for all in their communities. But I believe it is the church that is the one institution whose vocation is to implant and nurture this desire. It is the church in which we learn about the mutual responsibility we have for one another, where we witness the strength of our connectedness, and where we learn how to keep our covenant to bring about unity. It is the church that is being called in this time to develop and nurture leaders with a sense of character, calling, congruence, and commitment—a matrix that strengthens mission.

These qualities help prevent us from being shut up in the solitude of our own hearts. They enable us to move from isolation and insularity into caring and meaningful service to others. It is the church that helps to shape the habits of the mind and practices of the heart that prepare us to fulfill the Great Commission to baptize all nations, to respond to Christ's command to greet the stranger, tend the sick, provide for the poor, and feed the hungry. It is the vocation of lay and clergy leaders to create the conditions in which followers can learn how to live out genuinely responsible, ethical, and spiritual lives.

St. Luke's is a large Methodist church in Indianapolis, Indiana, eighty-six blocks north and several blocks east of Meridian Street, a major artery which connects north and south and intersects the center of the city, where Christ Church Cathedral is anchored. The landscape all along Meridian is dotted with significant historical homes and a variety of cultural, religious, service, and business institutions. Moving from the center of the city north through a notable neighborhood, one can see the rising towers and steeples of a diverse representation of mainline denominations—Trinity Episcopal Church at 33rd Street, North United Methodist Church at 38th Street, and Meridian Street Methodist Church another twenty blocks north. At the winding curve of 62nd Street, a majestic bell tower announces the presence of St. Paul's Episcopal Church, and at 71st and Meridian is the vast campus of Second Presbyterian Church, another large Protestant congregation.

Eleven blocks north and about a block west of this well-known city thoroughfare stands St. Luke's, on 86th Street, sharing a prominent place among these leading religious institutions. In the fourteen years that their minister, Dr. Kent Millard, has been at St. Luke's, the membership has doubled. When Kent arrived, church membership was thirty-eight hundred; currently, membership is over six thousand. Of the eleven hundred recently received members, seven hundred were unchurched! People join this church community because of the variety of worship offerings, the quality and diversity of preaching, the spiritual depth of educational offerings, its social justice outreach, and the music ministry.

Ten different services are offered every Sunday at three different locations, which include a dinner theater and an old renovated mansion. There are special services for adults, families, youth, and children. Youth in grades 1 through 6 help to plan and lead their services. Another innovative service, "Resonate," is specifically designed to attract Generation X members. This liturgy includes dialogue and more interaction than the traditional service.

The many outreach ministries provided by the church include singles groups and bereavement groups for children who have lost a parent or whose parents are divorced; Bible study groups; study circles on social issues; companion ministries with other churches; the adoption of a public school and a charter school; feeding and clothing ministries; and a center for spiritual exploration and healing. St. Luke's is a leader in community efforts to bridge relationships between blacks and whites through study circles on racism, and shared worship services and collaborative service projects with a local prominent African-American church.

"Something is always going on at St. Luke's" is a familiar characterization of the congregation. With a staff of sixty people, fifty of them full-time, and a budget of $3.5 million, it isn't difficult to see why this is a common description of the church. When the budget numbers are added to capital campaign contributions and special offerings, over $6 million "passes through the church" annually. A Strategic Planning and Policy Group composed of four key staff members and four key lay leaders meets with Kent weekly to review events and retain an awareness and understanding of the big picture, to cultivate the practice of being visionary, and to ensure congruence in their policy-making responsibilities. He then meets with all the clergy and program directors to strengthen the connection between the day-to-day activities, values, policies, and vision of the church.

Kent wisely takes time to rest, reflect, and engage in his inner work because he knows it affects the culture and his commitment to and practice of mission. He delegates well and takes a sabbath for personal development one day a month, and spends one day a week with his family.

When asked how he and St. Luke's have continued to thrive following the twenty-six-year pastorate of his predecessor, Kent's immediate response was, "I have a very low need to control people; I prefer to support them instead." This noncompetitive, cooperative, supportive attitude existed from the beginning. Upon his arrival at St. Luke's, he called up his predecessor and arranged to have breakfast with him. This initial meeting is now an ongoing practice. Instead of holding his predecessor at bay, he had the courage and confidence to reach out and learn from him. In the beginning he even shared with him the pastoral care responsibilities for members who had a long-standing relationship with the former minister.

A core belief that infuses policy and practice is that "everything and everyone that God has created has the spark of God within." Kent describes his role and that of other leaders in the church as helping others discover this spark and live their passion. To him, it is passion that drives the congregation. Using the metaphor of a car, Kent believes that passion is the energy or fuel that is essential for the car to run. "Vision is like the steering wheel, providing the focus and direction needed to get to the destination," he adds.

Kent suggests another essential element to the work of transformational leadership: teamwork. He has learned that when passion is evoked it drives involvement. Ministry in a large church can naturally lead to silo-building unless everyone intentionally remains connected and understands the importance of working together. Kent reinforces this through his remembering the vision and continually asking the question, "Where does God want to lead the church?" He believes the answer resides in the collective sharing of God's wisdom with each other.

The "spark of God" is metaphorical, and the practices emanating from this image have led to an impressive transformation in the church and the community it serves. It is invigorating to contemplate what a culture is like when everyone in the congregation feels that within themselves is the "spark of God"—the manifestation of God's existence in human form. The leadership in such an environment is an outward expression of an inward presence of the Divine—leadership as sacrament.

what is sacramental leadership?

According to the Catechism in the *Book of Common Prayer,* sacraments are "outward and visible signs of inward and spiritual grace." Leadership as sacrament embraces the skills and tasks of leading others as the embodiment and expression of faith. This kind of leadership is grounded in the knowledge that our very lives are a gift from God, a gift that came from the ultimate sacrifice, a gift to be shared with the world. The noted author on spirituality Tad Dunne writes, "Without faith, charity towards the neighbor washes away on the first rainy day. With faith, charity keeps surprising itself on how much self-sacrifice it is willing to endure and towards how many different people it is willing to pour out active, caring love."[1] Sacramental leadership pours out this active, caring love, rooted in a deep faith. It sees the congregation as the body of Christ, and all its actions as the *embodiment* of religious beliefs and core values expressed with congruence, authenticity, and integrity.

Sacramental leadership recognizes that we are all held in trust by a larger Love, transcendent of any particular clergy, lay leader, or congregation; a Love that connects all of us and that obligates us to care for one another. Leadership, seen and practiced as a sacrament, encourages this Love to flourish, creating and connecting a congregation that is in loving and faithful relationship with one another. The relationship between leaders and their followers is transformed because authority is shared, expectations and boundaries are clear, and mission and ministry is defined as including gifts from each order.

Leadership as sacrament integrates the different realms of our lives—the personal and the professional, the individual and the institutional, the private and the public, the subjective and the objective. It enables people to live out their lives "in whole cloth," to be fully who they are called to be—a spiritual practice in and of itself. A result is that our actions are more aligned with our words. Both shadow and light are acknowledged parts of the human condition, and their expression will not allow destructive energy to fester and grow.

The following are eight areas of practice that, if framed as a discipline of sacramental leadership, would be transformational.

THE SACRAMENTAL PRACTICE
OF STRATEGIC PLANNING

As most congregations know, planning for the future is simply good stewardship practice. Like any institution, churches must be fiscally responsible and exercise good fiduciary judgment, but unlike secular institutions, they must plan in service to a larger vision and vocation. Strategic planning can be an example of sacramental leadership. The decision to plan for the future is an act of faith, a statement of trust that in the coming together of human intent and Divine guidance we can influence the future and affect generations to come.

The sacramental practice of planning begins with historical reflection. Such reflection reveals the presence of the Divine in our lives and how it has been manifest in our lives and faith communities over time. Being aware of what and who has shaped us individually and corporately ingrains an awareness within us that as followers of Christ we are also followers of the cross—the ultimate symbol of transformation. Through the pain of death we will experience the joy of resurrection and we will be transformed; through suffering, we will be redeemed.

Sacramental leadership has the responsibility continually to tell the Story of both the institutional church and Scripture, and to create and sustain a culture and community of calling and action that is grounded in that Story. If as Frederick Buechner says, "God calls us to the place where our deep gladness and the world's deep hunger meet," a planning process can lead to an intersection of both the personal and corporate realms of our lives. The process needs to be infused with an openness to the unknown, a desire to serve God, and the knowledge that our beliefs are to be expressed in both word and deed. The sacramental leaders' approach to strategic planning begins with this theological grounding. What might the impact of the planning process be if it were to begin with Bible study? What if those responsible for the stewardship of the future began with hearing and discussing the story of the rich man who stored and hoarded his resources? Might this lead to an in-depth discussion of how easily we can idolize what is perishable and forget what is permanent? How easy it is to be captured by the illusion of control and be driven by a sense of scarcity rather than abundance? Such an approach could help planning committees to see again how fleeting the existence of possessions is and how constant is the existence of God's abundant love and unfailing grace.

Whatever planning process a parish might use, it has to be tethered to a much broader and deeper understanding of how what it produces will be "outward and visible signs of inward and spiritual grace." When planning is a practice of sacramental leadership, those involved will not be so obsessed with outcomes that they become more important than whether the process is one that creates a stronger, more cohesive, mission-based worshipping community, one that is well prepared to respond responsibly and ethically to the future. Such a process strengthens the faith and core values of a community. This approach does not preclude competent fund development, the establishment of reasonable financial goals, or the establishment of rigorous systems of accountability. It emphasizes the significance of matching who we say we are with what we actually do. Rather than giving the illusion that we have total control over the future, it positions congregations to see the fuller truth of their existence and to adapt to seismic change without losing the core of who they are. Whatever direction is decided, the parish and its leaders will be grounded in a knowledge of faith, and of their unique character and culture. Two examples of the sacramental practice of leadership follow.

THE SACRAMENTAL PRACTICE
OF LETTING GO

The rector of a twenty-year-old midwestern parish began to think about retirement several years before she would be canonically required to do so. She realized that her own planning process was intricately connected to the parish's need to begin strategic planning. Knowing that a conversation about this was imminent, she enlisted the assistance of a consultant, who helped her identify a group of congregational leaders to join with her in organizing and implementing the entire process. Each of the planning group's meetings began and ended with a moment of quiet reflection and prayer. The group agreed that the purpose of planning was to prepare for the transition in leadership and to ensure the health and vitality of the parish beyond the long tenure of the clergy leader.

The participation of all of the members in the congregation was sought through surveys, interviews, newsletters, and focus groups. Through this process, they identified major issues, concerns, and needs that needed to be addressed in the planning process. The planning group also canvassed leaders in the diocese and in their community, and pulled together a report of their findings for discussion and interpretation at a planning retreat.

A small subset of the group helped the rector to update the parish TimeScape.© At the retreat, a vast array of memorabilia—pictures, reports, and brochures that reflected past parish events—were displayed. Members signed in on the timeline and recalled their reasons for coming to the parish. In the planning retreat they each described significant internal and external events that affected and shaped the parish over time. This process enabled members to remember what they were seeking when they first came to the parish. Many spoke of looking for a spiritual home and identified the qualities and characteristics of the parish that drew them in and helped them to stay.

History is a source of identity which releases energy
when members of the congregation believe that
certain things must be done to live up to the
commitments of the past. —Carl Dudley

The reflection on their history revealed the parish's uniqueness and its capacity to respond to change over time. More importantly, it solidified the members' commitment to mission and strengthened their desire to be a community of faith dedicated to the spiritual support of members and potential members. The group was able to differentiate between physical growth and spiritual growth. Both were deemed to be important—physical growth could create the space in which their worship takes place, while spiritual growth creates and sustains the caring, cohesive community of faith.

The planning group was able to face its anxieties about the loss of their long-term clergy leader. They drew on their faith in something greater than themselves and realized their dependence on each other would help them discern what God was calling them to do and to be. They had the courage to be patient and prudent in their deliberations and to be pastoral in a very sensitive situation.

Through understanding planning as an action of the sacramental nature of leadership, the planning process increased this congregation's commitment and desire to strengthen its ministry. The rector and the congregation could begin to let go of one another in a constructive, life-giving way. Because they saw planning as a practice of sacramental leadership, and not just a technical exercise, the parish could start to celebrate the current rector's tenure, accept the departure, and begin the work of becoming spiritually prepared to call the next leader without infecting the search with fear or reactionary responses.

THE SACRAMENTAL PRACTICE
OF SPEAKING THE TRUTH IN LOVE

The second example of a church that engaged in a planning process led by leadership as a sacramental practice is an east-coast endowed parish. In 2003, this church found itself at the center of the post-General Convention controversy arising from the affirmation of the Diocese of New Hampshire's election of Gene Robinson, an openly gay bishop living in a same-sex relationship. In protest, six parishes in the diocese refused to send in their diocesan apportionments and also refused to have the bishop in the diocese confirm their youth.

The rector of this congregation, which was experiencing some of the tension and turmoil that other parishes were manifesting, refused to sit quietly during the tumult. Instead, he spoke of telling the truth and listening to one another in love; he spoke of reconciliation, while acknowledging the suffering of some and the joy of others. He immediately engaged lay leaders to work with him in the planning and development of a series of presentations and discussions on the issue. He worked with the lay chair of the adult education committee to frame the series theme around reconciliation, and made all of the sessions available to the general public. This gave the parish an opportunity to educate both themselves and a wider audience whose primary news source was CNN. The planning group was shaped and formed by prayer and periodically infused with theological education provided by the rector. Instead of withholding information that might have been in conflict with his own beliefs or might have caused more tension within the parish, he chose to present a variety of perspectives. The planning process itself led to intense discussions that permitted assertive but not aggressive exchanges, and allowed for passionate but not despotic statements.

When I met with the chair of the committee and the rector, I understood why their parish had not experienced the divisiveness that some others had. The committee's presentations to the congregation and the wider community had better equipped the parish to engage in difficult yet constructive conversations because the rector modeled this behavior. It certainly helped that the rector is a self-differentiated leader and a nonanxious presence in the midst of crises. His leadership conveyed the serious nature of the controversy without taking on the fears and anxieties ensconced in others. He also unhesitatingly supported the chair of the committee in her leadership role.

The importance of prayer was palpable. The postcommunion prayer from the Rite II service of Holy Eucharist captured their attitude toward each other:

Almighty and everliving God, we thank you for feeding us with the spiritual food of the most precious Body and Blood of your Son our Savior Jesus Christ; and for assuring us in these holy mysteries that we are living members of the Body of your Son, and heirs of your eternal kingdom. And now, Father, send us out to do the work you have given us to do, to love and serve you as faithful witnesses of Christ our Lord. To him, to you, and to the Holy Spirit, be honor and glory, now and for ever. Amen. (BCP 366)

Their work was sacramental and manifest in their organization and action.

When leadership is viewed as sacramental, we see the Divine in our interactions with others, and our meetings with others as encounters with the sacred mystery of incarnation. We are then able to adopt a discipline of beliefs and practices that allow us to:

* Envision what a healthy congregation looks like, and mutually identify and teach the habits and practices that will help to achieve this vision, which will enable the congregation to maintain health now and long beyond the tenure of current clergy.

* Ensure that the internal structural and operational systems and activities are aligned with the core values of the organization, thus building trust in the integrity of leadership and in the organization itself.

* See the parish as a living, breathing organism with the capacity for both health and illness, and be able to

identify and articulate warning signs—"symptoms"—of issues that pose a threat to the health and well-being of the system. This can be accomplished without dividing the congregation into camps "pro" and "con," or isolating those with whom there is conflict.

THE SACRAMENTAL PRACTICE OF READING REALITY

No matter how smart and sophisticated or capable a leader is, forming too quick an assessment of what underlies troubling symptoms can ultimately lead to work-avoidance and an abortion of the best solution or resolution. Leaders must always allow for other possible explanations that differ from their first conclusions.

Sacramental leaders can step back and gain a bigger view of a system and anticipate the impact that changes will have. It is difficult to see the whole when immersed in a myriad of day-to-day activities. Leaders engaged in transformational change are called to relinquish the managerial tendency to see only pieces and parts rather than the relationship between the parts. The geometric axiom that "the whole is greater than the sum of its parts" holds true for organizational systems.

When the vision is shared, it triggers inspiration, but its implementation becomes the greater challenge. Just as there is danger in pushing people too fast toward a goal to the point that integration of change does not happen, it is equally dangerous to think that once a vision is articulated the work is done. In fact, the point of agreement on a vision is when the real work begins. Keeping the energy and commitment of followers high at this point is paramount; and helping those involved to understand what and how they learned in the process will serve the organization well in accomplishing change in the future. As Peter Senge, author of *The Fifth Discipline,* says, "Most advocates of change focus on the changes they are trying to produce and fail to recognize the importance of learning capabilities." It is the learning capability of a congregation that will enable it to deal with future change and challenges in a healthy manner.

Sacramental leaders seek outside consultation and assistance in reading reality in times of stability and instability. They understand that the capacity to check their own perceptions and their effect on individuals and organizations minimizes the chances for internal eruptions. And when a crisis does occur, leaders and followers have the presence and patience to withstand the pressure to fix the problem before they really understand what the problem is.

THE SACRAMENTAL PRACTICE
OF INNER WORK

Since sacramental leadership is leadership that is based on self-knowledge, sacramental leaders must engage in the inner work of integrating being and doing. As Richard Niebuhr writes in *The Responsible Self,* "Self-knowledge is no mere luxury to be cultivated during idle moments. It is essential to the responsible life."

Leadership as sacrament recognizes that the primary instrument through which an organization can be freed to use its gifts and skills to change is the selfhood of the leader. It is the authenticity and integrity of a leader that engenders trust and confidence, and inspires shared responsibility and prudent action. These leaders are described as real and "down-to-earth" by followers. Identification with the leader helps followers to be more willing to engage in risk-taking and to do what is needed for the good of the group in spite of the possibility of failure.

There are multiple places in parish cultures where anxiety and fear lurk. What keeps these potentially corrosive emotions at a manageable level is a leader with a clear vision, an understanding of shadow and light, a connection to an overarching purpose, and the capacity to communicate focus and direction. These capacities provide a strong sense of security and meaning to followers.

The farther the outward journey takes you, the deeper the inner journey must be. — *Henri Nouwen*

Creating a community of learning and trust means developing a place in which individuals can risk being real and truthful, a psychologically and spiritually safe place where members feel a sense of belonging and are guided by the knowledge that there is something larger than their self-interest that must be considered. In this spiritually rich environment people can bring their whole selves for healing and growth.

THE SACRAMENTAL PRACTICE OF LEADING CHANGE

The sacramental leader understands the processes of change and selects and equips an internal "change team" to assist in bringing about the desired change. This kind of leadership helps develop these individuals into a cohesive group with a shared vision and a plan for strategic implementation of the vision. A planning or change team is united in its knowledge of parish history and of the character and culture of the organization. TimeScape© is one tool that engages individuals and communities of faith in a level of conversation that is informative and transformational. There are others that can help accomplish this goal as well. The lesson to be learned is that every organization has a history of responding to change, and knowing this history can assist the change team to intervene in ways that diminish anxiety and increase trust. It also is a reminder that change is not the enemy; denial that it exists or quick-fix responses are.

If the leader is a facilitator of change, problems are perceived as part of growth and ultimately solvable. In those situations in which the leader is resistive and reactionary, the message conveyed is a lack of confidence in the organization's internal capacity to deal with troublesome issues. The presenting symptoms of a problem can take on a life of their own, fueling more anxiety and enticing the leader to make unwise judgments and responses.

No matter how skilled leaders may be in communication, whatever they normally do will not be sufficient during complex change processes. In understanding the sacramental nature of leadership, they will find many and varied ways to send the desired message to followers that they want internalized and emulated. The leader lends clarity and consistency to the process. If the leader says the organization values open, honest opinions, then those who express themselves openly and honestly should be affirmed for this behavior. When the desired behavior happens, it should be immediately recognized and rewarded.

Sacramental leadership is not easy. It requires a high level of commitment, competence, confidence, and patience. In assuming this mantle leaders will be continually reminded that their real work is never finished. The real work is the development of a community of faith with the capacity to engage in actions and activities that are transformational.

Sacramental leadership is never a solo act. It involves a community of peers and followers committed to the vision, mission, and ministry of the church. The way this happens is through the practice of disciplines that lead to building trusting relationships and honest communication. The ability to create a community of trust and learning is key because the process of transformation is adaptive work, not a static, predictable sequential cycle.

THE SACRAMENTAL PRACTICE
OF MUTUAL MINISTRY

Sacramental leadership encourages the practice of mutual ministry, with leaders who truly believe that they have much to learn from others—both laity and clergy. The gifts and talents of many laity often lay untapped while clergy feel overworked, overextended, stressed, and burned out. The gifts of clergy can remain buried or underutilized if the laity hold on to rigid roles and stereotypes of who clergy are and what they "should" do.

The Reverend Brian Prior, who served as rector at the Episcopal Church of the Resurrection in Spokane, Washington, for twelve years, understands these practices well—he could have written them while leading his congregation through large-scale change. Brian was working as a diocesan staff member on congregational development when the bishop informed him of two troubled congregations and the possibility that they could become yoked. When this possibility turned into reality, Brian was asked if he would start the new church.

Wisdom is a state of the human mind and spirit characterized by deep understanding and profound insight. —Elisabeth Schüssler Fiorenza

---

He did what a leader who understands the sacramental nature and practices of leadership would do. Using the Baptismal Covenant as the core document to frame and guide the process, he engaged the congregation in an in-depth conversation about what they wanted their future to look like. During the listening process he began to hear alignment around a vision: the desire to be known in the community as "a place in which people are faith-fed in order to feed the world." The congregation wanted to be ministry-centered not clergy-centered, and Brian seized this as an opportunity to create a different model, something respectful of the parish history yet exemplary of freedom to choose a new future. His style of leadership is one of inquiry, and he asked multiple questions to bore down into the cultural level where core values—which are central to the work—reside.

He affirmed the challenges they faced and the successes shared during his stay. No matter what lay members did, Brian helped them to see that "everything contributes to the whole, and everything is ministry!" Whatever the service rendered, he would write a thank-you note acknowledging their ministry to the church and community. This parish flourished in spite of the crisis encountered after the General Convention of 2003, when it lost 12 percent of its members, and its pledge-and-plate revenues declined by 15 percent. When Brian arrived the average Sunday attendance was 70; now it is 175. There are five hundred members and the parish is fiscally sound. After only six years the mortgage will soon be burned. The spirit of the congregation is strong and their passion to serve is deep. Every year the annual meeting is held on Pentecost and the stewardship campaign begins in the spring; the dates are picked for their theological symbolism and meaning. These events are not isolated ritual and activity, they are the making of identity and calling. This is leadership-as-sacrament in practice.

Brian was the Vice President of the House of Deputies and was very active in the national church before being recently elected as bishop of the Diocese of Minnesota. As priest he was often absent for parish meetings, and the congregation seemed more willing than most to share his time with the larger church. When asked about what made this relationship and arrangement work, Brian quickly acknowledged the willingness of the congregation to live out a reality that is not normative, and spoke of the strength of its lay leadership. Perhaps this was because they understood their connection to the larger church and had the kind of mission partnership that is vital to effective ministry. Brian's exuberance, positive attitude, true appreciation of the gifts of all being used for the sake of ministry, and his solid belief in the importance of the gospel in action were also central to the vitality of this parish. The leadership and support of the diocesan bishop, who saw the need for a new type of parish and a new way of leading, were also keys to the success of this clergy-lay relationship.

This story is a reminder of several things. One is that the *being* of a leader is a critical factor in a transformation. Another is the significance of a leader with self-awareness and a vision of the preferred future. A leader does not always have to be the sole architect of the vision; in fact, his or her role may well be to listen for it within the congregation and then to take what is heard and enable the congregation to bring it to fruition. To do this means using the set of sacramental practices and skills already identified. One that has not yet been discussed but is recognized as necessary by all leaders who understand the sacramental nature of how they lead is the capacity to convene.

THE SACRAMENTAL PRACTICE OF CONVENING

Congregations are a complex mix of different people, with differences in perspective, education, knowledge, experience, skills, and economic condition. The leader's daunting task is to acknowledge and respect these differences and weld them into a community of a common vision and mission. The skill of convening is a critical practice in accomplishing this.

Convening consists of technical skills such as setting dates and times for meeting, selecting a location, and inviting participants. Developing an agenda, facilitating the proper attention on the right issues, sharing authority, ensuring accountability for task accomplishment, and setting up systems of sustainability are included. Effective leaders learn that these skills are the first order of response in building community. The complex and relational nature of his parish initially surprised Brian, and he quickly learned to use his understanding and knowledge of individual and group development to revitalize congregational ministry.

Whether the group has been in existence for some time or is just beginning, having an understanding of how and why it was formed, its developmental trajectory, and its underlying and operative values and assumptions will equip a leader to be most effective. Convening is a practice that is much more than just showing up; it requires considerable knowledge and preparation on the part of a leader. In order to convene there must be a basic knowledge of group development, group dynamics, and group process. The leader must know the history and composition of the group, know the norms and level of participation and its life in the parish, and use this information in planning the process of building relationships and trust. The historical research will reveal such facts as who envisioned and started the group; what the founding vision was and currently is; how it has evolved to date; what its achievements have been; and what its challenges are.

Knowledge of group development gives the leader an indication of what kind of interventions and behaviors will be most useful in its development. For example, in the early stages of a group's development it is appropriate for the leader to be more directive and to provide more structure. This is usually done by clearly communicating the purpose of the group, its goals, objectives, and desired outcomes. Clear expectations of membership are stated to help people decide whether they can invest and commit. Norms are made explicit to ensure respectful, constructive conversation. An example of group norms we use can be found on the following pages.

GROUP NORMS

1. *Begin and end on time.*
Whatever times the group has established, they will agree to honor. If it looks as though they cannot do so, they will renegotiate.

2. *Each person is actively engaged.*
Those who attend are committing to a deep level of involvement in the process, which will require listening, paying attention to what is going on, and being actively engaged. This allows each person to participate in the ways they are most comfortable while being cognizant that how they choose to partici-pate positively or detrimentally affects the group as a whole. This also reminds the group of the variety of ways that people can contribute and participate—everyone does not have to talk, and everyone shares at their level of comfort.

3. *Be open, honest, and direct.*
Communication in the group needs to be an open and honest process if the group engages in real work. Each participant is committing to behavior that will create an environment in which this level of conversation can occur by modeling direct, honest feedback themselves.

4. *Use "I" messages.*
This is a corollary to number 3, and provides an important way to honor that norm. Using "I" messages helps each participant to own responsibility for their own thoughts, ideas, and feeling. This does not permit people to speak for others or to hide behind what others may feel or think.

5. *Be respectful of differences.*
Each person brings his or her own distinctive history of experiences and perspectives to this experience, and it is important to acknowledge and respect this in the course of conversation. We are asking participants to listen and respond respectfully, seeking to understand but not necessarily to agree.

6. *Attend and prepare for all sessions.*
This is essential to a group if they wish to fully benefit from this experience. Assignments are to be honored.

7. *We all have expertise.*
Everyone has considerable knowledge and skill; it is important for us to remember this and create ways in which it can be utilized. This norm diminishes the chances of entrenched hierarchies in a group to remain established and invites the participation of all.

8. *We are responsible for our own learning.*
This norm is very similar to number 6, but broader. This is a contract with the group to help form the educational experience and to shape what occurs in the session. Participants are asked to speak up if they have questions, concerns, or suggestions or if they are feeling lost or disconnected. The opportunity to renegotiate their experience is always available.

9. *We will keep information confidential.*
Everything shared in the group remains in the group. If an individual wishes to discuss their own experience, they can but they are asked not to share what others said, did, or decided without the person's consent.

10. *No beepers or telephones.*
Participants will find the educational experience far more beneficial if the group is not subject to continual interruptions or external diversions. The focus needs to be on the work at hand, and the group needs to know that there is shared focus and commitment and a stability to the membership as they deal with difficult issues.

11. *We can stop the process and confer.*
This is a norm that allows for anyone to stop the process and ask for clarification or renegotiation of activities based on time or need considerations. This permits a certain level of creative flexibility necessary in good pedagogy. It also heightens participants' ownership and sense of responsibility for what is going on in the training.

12. *Serious work can also be fun.*
This is not a command, but an invitation and reminder. As one of my mentors reminds us, "This is a serious business, but it need not be a deadly one!" The leader needs to pay attention to creating the space and environment for an element of playfulness and humor to happen.

Every group establishes rules for how it wants to operate. To a stranger they may be unspoken and discovered only through experience. If a leader observes that a group becomes silent in the presence of conflict or that it rushes to judgment or makes decisions quickly, he or she is observing group norms. Leaders help groups make their norms for behavior explicit and lead them to examine, evaluate, comply with, and/or modify them when needed.

Through observation the leader learns whether a group is in the first stage of development, during which issues of inclusion and exclusion predominate, or if they are in a later phase of resolving issues of power and control or negotiating levels of desired relationships. Any one of these phases is instructive to the leaders and influence the behaviors assumed. I recall working with Ann Smith and a team of consultants in the Women in Mission and Ministry Leadership Development Initiative, which reached hundreds of women leaders across the country. In almost every instance we could track the group's need to claim its authority on the second day of the five-day experience. When this phase of development occurred we were able to help the group and its members to own their authority and learn to use it constructively. Our ability to handle this phase of development prevented an escalation of defensiveness, rebellion, scapegoating, or attack on the leaders—all of which divert groups from engaging in their real work. Weak or uninformed leadership that lacks the knowledge of how groups develop and behave causes more difficulties at this point. Such ignorance contributes to repressing the group's struggle with becoming more mature in its functions. If the leader responds in an authoritarian, top-down manner in order to reassert or regain control, emotions are driven underground. Things may appear to be under control in the short-term, but in the long-term repression will only intensify issues and the emotions, turning them into a tinder box of conflict. The leader may mistake a group's silence or passivity as compliance or resolution. When Brian saw such signs as these in his congregation, everyone knew he would comment and question what was going on.

We have all heard of instances in which there is member dissatisfaction in parishes. If the leaders respond aggressively, the members can move into repression or regression but the memory of discontent remains, ready to add fuel to another incident later. Creating a community of trust and learning requires the cultivation of a culture of dialogue and an ability to engage others in deep conversation. When group members feel they can speak their opinions freely and disagree without fear of retribution, trust grows.

When "hospitable space for disciplined reflection" is created, a climate of psychological trust and safety is established so that group members can feel free to share their thoughts and feelings without fear of violation of confidentiality. When members can trust that what they say will remain in the group and will not be used against them, they feel able to risk being open and honest. The way to help people learn this is to provide a space in which they can voice their opinion and beliefs and also be open to the opinions and beliefs of others without being ostracized or chastised. This is the practice of leadership as sacrament.

The chart on the following page can assist leaders in identifying when they are working on a technical or adaptive aspect of an issue. This model can be used as a tool to examine a parish's preferred model of ministry.

MODELS OF MINISTRY©

	CORPORATE MODEL		MINISTRY MODEL
FOCUS	Metrics	←→	Mission
SKILLS	Technical	←→	Adaptive
GUIDED BY	Strategic planning	←→	Prayerful discernment
PROGRAM DEVELOPMENT	Competitive	←→	Collaborative
GOAL	Growth	←→	Connection
STRUCTURE	Hierarchical	←→	Circular
LEADERSHIP	Authority, status, power	←→	Altruism, trusteeship, passion
CONGREGANTS	Resources for deployment	←→	Resources for development

While the practice, disciplines, and models sound easy, their implementation is complicated by the fact that human behavior is complex, organic, and, at times, unpredictable. This means the leader must always be both observer and participant. What the leader sees and hears will guide whether, when, and how to respond. A key skill of sacramental leadership is the appropriate timing of an intervention. The leader can usually tell when the timing is optimum because the response of the individual or group is less defensive, the real issue surfaces, the entire group is engaged, the conversation is open, and the group moves forward in the real work it must accomplish. The art of reading the group while also mobilizing it to accomplish its work is sacramental leadership. The leader ensures that the diversity of opinion and the wide range of thoughts are expressed and given respectful consideration in discussion and decision-making.

The context, processes, and tools for leadership as sacrament are transformational. They help leaders know when to use technical and adaptive skills. They are able to read the surface and the depth of issues and of parish culture, lead an array of groups through the phases of change, and create communities of learning and trust through modeling authentic leadership and using their knowledge of group development.

---

summary

*"And now, Father, send us out to do the work
you have given us to do."*

This desire to serve expressed in the Rite II postcommunion prayer is the heart of sacramental leadership. These are our marching orders, and they convey the notion of leadership as a sacramental act of faithful witness, love, and service that brings honor and glory to God.

The Episcopal Church is at a crevice in history, a crease in time when it is being called to reset and restate in new ways who we are and why we exist. We are being called to identify what we can contribute to resolving the turbulence within and without in transformational ways. We are being called to be a credible and authentic example of Christian faith. We are to exemplify congruence in our beliefs and actions. Our ability to influence and exercise power will be revealed through authentic behavior and integrity of being. Sacramental leadership is rooted in tenets and practices familiar to the readers of this book and found in the previous volumes in this series. There has never been another time in which the potential of the Episcopal Church to change and to lead has been needed more. Our Baptismal Covenant must be the standard for how we work together inside the church and out in the world. We can no longer thrive in top-down stratifications of entitlement in which power *over* rather than power *with* predominates. Leadership as sacrament is our ministry. Information must be accessible to all, and core values must be clearly articulated and aligned with our actions. We cannot sequester people in beautiful spaces of worship, music, and liturgy without also engaging them in deeper reflection on identity and character, calling and congruence. We can practice prayerful silence *and* embrace responsible action.

Robert Kennedy's words remind us that "few will have the greatness to bend history itself; but each of us can work to change a small portion of events, and in the total of all those acts will be written the history of this generation. All we need is courageous leadership." We have this kind of leadership and the potential for more of it exists in the church. Our task is to elicit the "spark of God" and through intentional education and development of clergy and lay leadership set the church ablaze with the passion of the Christian vocation. When we do, reality will shift and all things will be transformed. May we have the courage to heed our call.

Nothing that is worth doing
can be achieved in our lifetime;
*   therefore we must be saved by hope.*
Nothing which is true or beautiful or good
makes complete sense in any immediate context of history;
*   therefore we must be saved by faith.*
Nothing we do, however virtuous,
can be accomplished alone;
*   therefore we must be saved by love.*
                                        —*Reinhold Neibuhr*

A Guide for
Discussion

You may of course read the books in this series on your own, but because they focus on the transformation of the Episcopal Church in the twenty-first century the books are especially useful as a basis for discussion and reflection within a congregation or community. The questions below are intended to generate fruitful discussion about leadership within the congregations and national churches with which members of the group are familiar.

Each group will identify its own needs and will be shaped by the interests of the participants and their comfort in sharing personal life stories. Discussion leaders will wish to focus on particular areas that address the concerns and goals of the group, using the questions and themes provided here simply as suggestions for a place to start the conversation.

chapter one

A Time of No Longer and Not Yet

In this chapter Katherine Tyler Scott sets the context for changes in church leadership required in the twenty-first century. She believes that "shared ministry between clergy and laity can be an enlivening force" in the church today, especially when church leaders offer a "clear, shared vision, can listen respectfully to one another, can invite participation from everyone, and exhibit congruence between word and deed" (pp. 7–8).

✦ What has been your experience of "shared ministry between clergy and laity" in the congregations and dioceses of which you have been a part?

✦ What are some of the ways church leaders can offer "a clear, shared vision" of a congregation's mission and ministry?

✦ What are some of the concrete ways church leaders can "listen to one another" and "invite participation from everyone"? How is such listening and participation sometimes discouraged?

✦ How do church leaders "exhibit congruence between word and deed" in your congregation or diocese? What are the consequences when words and deeds do not match?

✦   ✦   ✦   ✦   ✦

The author notes that according to one study, "The leadership style of the priest determines a congregation's perception of the roles and responsibilities of clergy, church staff, and laity. It is clergy leadership that enables a congregation to form and strengthen itself as a community and to understand the larger context in which parish life exists" (p. 4).

◆ Do you agree with this assessment of the importance of clergy leadership in Episcopal congregations? Why or why not?

◆ What has been your experience of various leadership styles of clergy in the congregations of which you have been a part?

◆ In your experience, how does the leadership style of the clergy affect the roles of other leaders in the congregation, including church staff, vestry members, committee members, and other lay leaders?

chapter two

Shifting Paradigms

In this chapter the author describes "the changing paradigm of leadership," noting that congregations today are seeking spiritual leadership to guide the search for meaning and significance so widespread today. She notes: "The very charism that once distinctly defined the Episcopal Church is precisely what so many people are seeking: the ability to embrace uncertainty and ambiguity responsibly. In other words, the spiritual search is for the development of character, the identification of calling, the alignment between belief and behavior, and the opportunity to make a significant contribution to the world" (p. 22).

◆ In what ways have various church leaders helped you with character development and a deeper understanding of your baptismal vocation and identity?

♦ How has the church supported your efforts to create an "alignment between belief and behavior" in your daily life?

♦ How has the church informed and strengthened your desire to make a contribution to the well-being of others in your community and in the world?

♦   ♦   ♦   ♦   ♦

In her discussion of the top-down paradigm for leadership versus a paradigm based on relationship, the author asks several difficult questions that must be addressed in order for transformation to take place (see pages 32–33). With your particular congregation or diocese in mind, how would you respond to her questions:

♦ What can the church learn from the past that will enable it to strengthen its financial health and change a downward trend in growth and giving?

♦ What will need to change in the content, teaching methodology, and preparation of the next generation in order for this group to effectively occupy the leadership positions that will be open in the near future?

♦ How will the next generation of leaders be best prepared to assume the governance and leadership responsibilities essential to the survival and future vitality of the Episcopal Church?

♦ What will the operating paradigm for congregational life and leadership need to be, in order to have a spiritually strong and healthy parish?

chapter three

On the Margin: Promise and Possibility

In this chapter the author states: "Being on the margin can be seen as a place of loss and powerlessness, a void in which nothing happens and where no one can make a difference. But being on the margin can be more than a state of loss; it can be a place of transformation" (p. 47).

♦ When have you experienced "being on the margin" in your own life? in your parish?

♦ In what ways was the experience of being marginalized an experience of loss for you? for your parish?

♦ In what ways have you experienced the margin as "a place of transformation" in your own life? in your parish?

♦ ♦ ♦ ♦ ♦

The author believes that "being on the margin means having a changed perspective that comes from being dislocated from a position of centrality" (p. 48).

♦ How has your congregation's perspective needed to change in order to adapt to the reality of the mainline church's movement to the margins of modern society?

♦ In what ways has the "location" of your church congregation within the structures and activities of the wider community changed over the years since its founding?

"Being on the margin," the author notes, "can change the church's perspective on and strategies for growth" (p. 49).

+ Has your congregation grown or shrunk in size since its founding? What are some of the factors that influenced the change in size?

+ How is "growth" viewed in your congregation?

+ What do you make of Malcolm Warford's observation that we "often get bigger because we aren't able to choose what really claims us" (p. 50)? In what ways has that been true of your congregation?

◆ ◆ ◆ ◆ ◆

"Being on the margin is a place of many opportunities and options, and it is easy to be pulled in many directions," the author notes. "Having a clear aim can help followers get through difficult or challenging circumstances and to emerge with strength and joy" (pp. 52–53).

+ Describe an occasion in which the statement of a clear aim by church leaders was able to strengthen your resolve and help you or your congregation through a difficult situation. How was that "clear aim" communicated?

+ When you recall an occasion in which the failure to hold and/or communicate a clear aim led to fragmentation and division, can you identify the points at which church leaders failed to clarify the vision? What caused them to be silent at those points?

♦ ♦ ♦ ♦ ♦

When churches are on the margin in terms of the life of the spirit, they can become places of "reaching for a fuller and deeper understanding of issues." The author comments that this spiritual margin is "not a neat, orderly, antiseptic place"; rather, as the birthplace of "a new order," it is "organic, messy, and unpredictable"—and the "fertile ground for redefinition and renewal" (p. 54).

♦ In what ways is your congregation living "on the margin" spiritually? Would you describe your spiritual life as "organic, messy, and unpredictable," or more on the "neat and orderly" end of the spectrum?

♦ In what ways is your congregation afraid to embrace life "on the margin," and instead chooses to remain where it has been in the past? Where do you see courageous members of the congregation exploring new paths and finding them to be "fertile ground for redefinition and renewal"?

chapter four

The Call: Leadership as Vocation

In this chapter Katherine Tyler Scott focuses on the ways the covenant we make at our baptism, in its call for mutual ministry, forms a "template for the relationship and responsibilities of laity and clergy" (p. 57).

♦ Describe some of the ways mutual ministry is lived out in your own life. Where do you see it in your congregation, diocese, and national church?

♦ Where is such an understanding of shared ministry lacking, in your view?

Knowing a congregation's "organizational culture" is often an important first step to a deeper understanding of its mission and purpose. Review the chart summarizing some of the key components of an organization's culture provided on page 60, and consider the various "levels" of your congregation's underlying structures and assumptions.

♦ *Artifactual:* What do you remember as the important points in your parish's history? Why did you join the congregation? What do the "artifacts" of your congregation—the building, the worship space, the service bulletins, the newsletters—tell others about your congregation?

♦ *Structural and Behavioral:* How would you respond to the questions listed on page 65 about coffee hour in your congregation? What do your answers tell you about patterns of communication and community life in your parish?

♦ *Philosophical:* What are some of the "unquestioned assumptions and unchallenged core beliefs and values" of your congregation? How are they expressed in your worship or congregational life?

♦ *Foundational:* Where are the points of "disconnect" in which the foundational beliefs of your congregation do not match its actions? In your view, what work needs to be done to "realign" these beliefs and actions? If it is true, as Fredrica Harris Thompsett has said, that "*what* we choose to notice reveals *who* we are" (pp. 73–74), then what do the people, issues, and activities your congregation focuses most of its energy and attention on tell you about the identity and mission of the congregation? What (or who) do you think is missing or neglected?

◆　◆　◆　◆　◆

The author believes that change is the constant and new reality that leaders must confront. She introduces a three-phase model for change that describes what happens when organizations deal with change structurally and emotion-ally (p. 79). The transforming leader must be aware of both, and be able to manage them.

◆ What have been the significant changes in the life of your parish in the past ten years?

◆ How have these changes affected your parish?

◆ How have your lay and clergy leaders handled these changes in the congregation? In what ways were they able to help the congregation move from initial denial through the confusion of being in "The Gap" and then into an acceptance and embracing of new life?

◆ What have you learned through this experience of change about your capacity to adapt and be trans-formed?

chapter five

The Sacramental Nature of Leadership

In this chapter the author notes that the church is one of the few institutions in which we are able to develop our sense of mutual responsibility for the quality of life for all in our communities. In the church we can be encouraged to nurture our sense of "character, calling, congruence, and commitment" (p. 86).

♦ How has the church helped you to live out your baptismal calling to serve others in the name of Christ, both in the congregation and in your daily life and work?

♦ How has the church provided support and encouragement in your ministries of compassion and your efforts to improve the quality of life for all? When has that support been lacking or misdirected? How have you been able to provide that support for others?

♦ ♦ ♦ ♦ ♦

The author identifies "strategic planning" as one way that sacramental leadership can be manifested in the church (p. 91).

♦ Reflect on your experience of strategic planning— perhaps in vestry meetings, committee meetings, annual parish meetings, diocesan conventions, or worship planning meetings—as a manifestation of sacramental leadership in your congregation or diocese. How have the plans made at those meetings expressed the "vision and vocation" of your congregation?

♦ How have you experienced your own practice of leadership as a sacrament—a visible sign of spiritual grace?

♦ Reflect on Frederick Buechner's insight that "God calls us to the place where our deep gladness and the world's deep hunger meet." How would you describe your congregation's "deep gladness"? Where do you see the world's "deep hunger" most urgently? What are some of the places they meet in your congregation's mission and ministry today?

♦ ♦ ♦ ♦ ♦

Reflect on the "Models of Ministry" matrix found on page 110, focusing on your experience as a committee member offering leadership in your congregation during the past year or two.

♦ What would you say has been the primary model of ministry exercised in the committee? Why?

♦ Was that model effective and helpful in supporting the mission of the committee? Why or why not?

♦ How was conflict or disagreement handled in the group? Who provided guidance in efforts of reconciliation when needed?

♦ Did the leadership regularly provide a "hospitable space for disciplined reflection" (p. 109)? If not, why not?

♦ How were the goals of the group defined, clarified, and supported by the leadership?

♦ What were some of the failures in leadership for the group? How were these handled?

◆ ◆ ◆ ◆ ◆

The author concludes, "The Episcopal Church is at a crevice in history, a crease in time when it is being called to reset and restate in new ways who we are and why we exist. We are being called to identify what we can contribute to resolving the turbulence within and without in transformational ways. We are being called to be a credible and authentic example of Christian faith. We are to exemplify congruence in our beliefs and actions. Our ability to influence and exercise power will be revealed through authentic behavior and integrity of being" (p. 111).

   ◆ Do you agree with her assessment of where the Episcopal Church and other mainline churches find themselves today?

   ◆ How would you describe the contribution we are being called to make in "resolving the turbulence within and without in transformational ways"?

Resources

websites and organizations

There are some excellent sites and resources on leadership and transformation available on the internet. They are, however, a "moving target," with information changing regularly.

INTERNATIONAL LEADERSHIP ASSOCIATION
www.ila.-net.org
University of Maryland
1119 Taliaferro / College Park, Maryland 20724-7715
The International Leadership Association is the global network for all those who practice, study, and teach leadership. The ILA promotes a deeper understanding of leadership knowledge and practices for the greater good of individuals and communities worldwide.

KI THOUGHTBRIDGE, LLC
www.kithoughtbridge.com
135 North Pennsylvania Street, Suite 1750
Indianapolis, Indiana 46204

KI ThoughtBridge, LLC is a company noted for an integrated approach to leadership development, change management, conflict resolution, and mediation. The company works with leaders in business, philanthropy, and education to develop adaptive leadership skills that enable the transformation of individuals, institutions, and communities. KI ThoughtBridge is based in Indianapolis, Indiana, with offices in Cambridge, Massachusetts, and Denver, Colorado.

---

b o o k s

Bass, Dorothy C. *Practicing Our Faith: A Way of Life for a Searching People.* San Francisco: Jossey-Bass, 1997.
   Contributing authors provide theological and practical wisdom about ways to integrate our faith beliefs into everyday actions.

Bohm, David. *On Dialogue.* New York: Routledge, 1996.
   The classic on the elements of true dialogue in a world that is witnessing a breakdown in meaningful communication.

Bridges, William. *Transitions: Making Sense of Life's Changes.* Twenty-fifth anniversary edition. Cambridge, Mass.: Da Capo Press, 2004.
   Drawing on anthropology, sociology and the author's professional experience, Bridges identifies and describes the universal phases of change and transformation.

Brown, Judy. *A Leader's Guide to Reflective Practice.* Victoria, British Columbia: Trafford Publishing, 2008.
   A teaching guide that models the subject itself and demonstrates the value of reflection in leadership.

Buechner, Frederick. *Listening To Your Life: Daily Meditations With Frederick Buechner.* San Francisco: HarperOne, 1992.
   Inspirational writings for daily meditation, connecting what seems to be mundane to what we consider sacred.

Chait, Richard P., Thomas P. Holland, Barbara E. Taylor. *The Effective Board of Trustees*. New York: MacMillan Publishing Company, 1991.
The authors share six dimensions of effective governance leadership based on their extensive research and findings.

Conger, Jay, and associates. *Spirit at Work: Discovering the Spirituality in Leadership*. San Francisco: Jossey-Bass, 1994.
This is a series of essays by a variety of writers committed to developing whole, healthy leaders.

De Caussade, Jean-Pierre. *The Sacrament of the Present Moment*. New York: Harper and Row, 1982.
A beautiful exegeses of our relationship to God and how our acknowledgment of and attentiveness to this reality enriches our identity and presence in the world.

Eliade, Mircea. *The Sacred and the Profane: The Nature of Religion*. Orlando, Florida: Harcourt Brace Jovanovich, 1987.
Introduces the meaning of religion in humankind from ancient to modern times and offers a historical trajectory of attempts to make meaning out of the mystery of Christianity.

Friedman, Edwin H. *A Failure of Nerve: Leadership in the Age of the Quick Fix*. New York: Church Publishing, Inc., 1999.
A prophetic resource identifying the lack of courage in leadership and the impact on religious systems. Its wisdom and insights are invaluable to those leading large-scale change.

Heifetz, Ronald A. *Leadership Without Easy Answers*. Boston: Belknap Press of Harvard University, 1994.
This landmark book distinguishes between the technical and adaptive challenges that leaders face, and provides a process by which the leader can engage individuals and institutions in their real work.

Jones, Michael. *Artful Leadership: Awakening the Commons of the Imagination*. Bloomington, Ind.: Trafford Publishing, 2006.
This book is a gem on transformational leadership in which the musician and author weaves together individual consciousness and connection with character and the commons.

LeVoy, Gregg. *Callings: Finding and Following an Authentic Life.* New York: Three Rivers Press, 1997.
One of the most inspirational books written about human purpose and finding the unique reason for one's existence.

Lippit, Gordon, and Ronald Lippit. *The Consulting Process in Action.* Second edition. San Francisco: Pfieffer, 1994.
A key resource for internal and external consultants engaged in organizational development work.

Madsen, Richard, William Sullivan, Ann Swidler, and Steve M. Tipton. *Habits of the Heart.* Los Angeles: University of California Press, 1985.
A study of what motivates people to serve others and observations about why such service is in danger of declining.

Niebuhr, H. Richard. *The Responsible Self: An Essay in Christian Moral Philosophy.* San Francisco: Harper, 1963.
A beautifully written deep exploration of what Christian life looks like when based on an understanding of moral and ethical sensibilities.

Nouwen, Henri J. M. *Life of the Beloved: Spiritual Living in a Secular World.* New York: Crossroads Publishing Company, 1992.
A journey into the nature of our spiritual life and relationship to God through writings to a friend.

Palmer, Parker J. *The Company of Strangers: Christians and the Renewal of America's Public Life.* New York: Crossroads Publishing Company, 1981.
Explores and expands the meaning of public and the conditions that erode and enrich it, giving an urgency to the need to bridge the inner and outer realms of our lives.

Rogers, Carl R. *On Becoming a Person: A Therapist's View of Psychotherapy.* Boston: Houghton Mifflin Company, 1961.
A pioneering work on the development of human beings and the creation of opportunities/experiences/context in which the real self is formed, can evolve, and may be revealed.

Schein, Edgar H. *Organizational Culture and Leadership*. San Francisco: Jossey-Bass, 1985.
The best expert on culture and leadership provides a dynamic model for exploring the complexities and context for understanding how leaders create and change culture.

Smith, David H. *Entrusted: The Moral Responsibilities of Trusteeship*. Bloomington, Ind.: Indiana University Press, 1995.
The description of the moral duties of trusteeship are applicable to those of leadership. Three core principles that constitute the key responsibilities are identified.

Toms, Michael, and Justine Willis Toms. *True Work*. New York: Bell Tower/Crown Publishing Company, 1998.
A story of discovering one's true calling and integrating one's values in the workplace.

Tyler Scott, Katherine. *Creating Caring and Capable Boards: Reclaiming the Passion for Active Trusteeship*. San Francisco: Jossey-Bass, 2000.
This essay describes the philosophy of a depth education for board leaders. It describes how institutions can be brought into a deeper alignment with their highest purpose.

Tyler Scott, Katherine. *The Integrated Work of Leadership*. Indianapolis: Ki ThoughtBridge, 2006.
This workbook is based on a model that integrates the technical and adaptive skills of leaders with their inner and outer work. A series of exercises helps the leader to further develop the practices and discipline of adaptive leadership. The workbook includes brief essays, reflections, quotes, and a journal that inspires leaders to understand the sacramental nature of their actions.

Tyler Scott, Katherine. *Trusteeship: Developing Self, Organizations and Community*. Lilly Endowment Leadership Education Program, 1990.
Focuses on trusteeship, a unique concept that has transformed the responsibilities of governance, leadership, and fiduciary practices.

Notes and Sources

---

notes

NOTES TO CHAPTER 1

1. From a presentation by Dr. Diogenes Allen, "Spiritual Awakenings," at the Consortium of Endowed Episcopal Parishes Conference, 1993.

2. L. Ann Hallisey, Thomas P. Holland, Susan Page Johnson, William L. Sachs, *The Search for Coherence: Soundings on the State of Leadership Among Episcopalians* (New York: Episcopal Church Foundation, 2003),12. See http://www.episcopalfoundation.org/ resource/Resource%20Library/Search%20for%20Coherence/ SearchforCoherence.pdf

3. Carl S. Dudley, David A. Roozen, *Faith Communities Today: Report on Religion in the United States Today,* Hartford Institute for Religion Research (March 2001), 8. The entire FACT survey report may be found at http://fact.hartsem.edu/research/fact2000/ Final%20FACTrpt.pdf.

4. Keith Brown, "Some Key Data and Trends in the Episcopal Church," presented to the Church Pension Group board in 2007.

5. Kirk Hadaway, "Is the Episcopal Church Growing (or Declining)?"; www.episcopalchurch.org/documents/2004GrowthReport(1).pdf.

6. See, for example, Matthew Price's report "Church Trends and Policy Initiatives," Church Pension Group, 2007.

NOTES TO CHAPTER 2
1. Jeffery Sheller, "Faith in America," *U.S. News and World Report* (May 6, 2002).
2. Parker J. Palmer, *To Know As We Are Known* (New York: HarperCollins, 1993), 22.
3. Fredrica Harris Thompsett, *We Are Theologians: Strengthening the People of the Episcopal Church* (Cambridge, Mass.: Cowley Publications, 1989), 60.

NOTES TO CHAPTER 4
1. Edgar Schein, *Organizational Leadership and Culture,* second edition, (San Francisco: Jossey-Bass, 1992), 17.

NOTES TO CHAPTER 5
1. Tad Dunne, *Lonergan and Spirituality: Towards a Spiritual Integration* (Chicago: Loyola University Press, 1985), 123.

---

sources quoted

Quotations set apart within the chapters have been taken from the following books and articles.

Warren Bennis, *On Becoming a Leader* (Reading, Mass.: Addison-Wesley, 1989).

Bruno Bettelheim, *The Uses of Enchantment* (New York: Vintage Books, 1975, 1989).

Frederick Buechner, *Wishful Thinking: A Seeker's ABC* (San Francisco: HarperSanFrancisco, 1993).

Carl Dudley, *The Trustee Educator,* vol. 1 (TLD Inc., 1990)

Eric Erikson, *Childhood and Society* (New York: W. W. Norton, 1993).

Elisabeth Schüssler Fiorenza, *Wisdom Ways: Introducing Feminist Biblical Interpretation* (Maryknoll, N.Y.: Orbis Books, 2001).

Edwin H. Friedman, *A Failure of Nerve: Leadership in the Age of the Quick Fix* (New York: Church Publishing, 2007).

John Gardner, *On Leadership* (New York: The Free Press, 1990).

Michael Jones, *Artful Leadership: Awakening the Commons of the Imagination* (Bloomington, Ind.: Trafford Publishing, 2006).

H. Richard Niebuhr, *The Responsible Self* (New York, Harper and Row, 1963).

Henri Nouwen, *Jesus: A Gospel* (Maryknoll, N.Y.: Orbis Books, 2001).

Henri Nouwen, *The Way of the Heart* (New York: Ballentine Books, 1981).

Parker J. Palmer, *The Company of Strangers* (New York: Crossroads Publishing, 1981).

Katherine Tyler Scott, *The Integrated Work of Leadership* (Indianapolis: KiThoughtBridge, 1994, 2006.

Fredrica Harris Thompsett, *We Are Theologians: Strengthening the People of the Episcopal Church* (Cambridge, Mass.: Cowley Publications, 1989).